Trial of

# *Billy Byrne*

## of Ballymanus

Dee-Jay Publications wish to record their thanks to
the County Development Team of

Wicklow
County
Council

whose major contribution towards production costs
made this book possible.

Dee-Jay Publications

This edition published by

# Dee-Jay Publications
3 Meadows Lane
Arklow
Co. Wicklow
Ireland

First published by William McKenzie, 33 College Green, Dublin
(No date given, but circa 1799)

Foreword © Jim Rees, 1996
ISBN 0 9519239 2 7

Cover:   Billy Byrne Monument, Market Square, Wicklow
Photograph by Peter Kearns

Printed by Colour Books Ltd., Dublin

# PUBLISHER'S NOTE

This account of the trial of Billy Byrne was first published by William McKenzie of Dublin shortly after the event. In re-publishing it, we have decided to tamper with the text as little as possible. Original spellings have been retained, even where they contradict themselves (e.g. Byrne, in the course of his defence, referring to Bridget Doolin as Bridget Dolan; Bridget Meagher's name also appearing as Mahar; the forms Mergan, Mergen and Mergin being interchangeable). We have resisted the temptation to standardise in order to retain the 'immediacy' of the text. We have, however, made slight adjustments to punctuation where commonsense and clarity demanded. For the same reason, some blocks of text have been paragraphed. We have also added an index and included the ballad "Billy Byrne of Ballymanus". The inclusion of the ballad is to illustrate the popular image of Billy Byrne and certainly not for its literary qualities. In a very few instances, the text appears to 'jump' from one line of questioning to another (e.g. when questioning John Hopkins - p.28 - Byrne's last question appears totally out of context). Also, there are occasional references to testimony of witnesses whose evidence was not recorded in McKenzie's published version. In such instances we have simply remained faithful to that version.

# FOREWORD

The year 1798 was one of rebellion in various parts of Ireland. There were three major theatres loosely linked through the activities of the Society of United Irishmen, but each was distinct from the other two. In May, June and into July, there were two fronts. The 'Antrim Rebellion' raged in the extreme north-east of the country, while the 'Wexford Rebellion' affected Wicklow, Carlow, Kildare, Meath, and, to a lesser extent, Waterford. After these insurrections had been crushed, a third, belated uprising took place in Mayo, aided by long-promised troops from Napoleonic France. This, too, was put down with comparative ease and vengeful brutality.

Each of these regional conflicts burned their way into history and, perhaps more importantly, into folklore. Over the following decades, fact fused with fiction making man and myth inseparable. Acts of bravery, and of cowardice, assumed Homeric proportions. Both sides glossed over atrocities committed in their names and painted as black and brutal a picture as possible of their enemies.

One hundred years later, at the end of the nineteenth century, there was a renewed sense of nationalism and nationality sweeping Ireland. The Gaelic League was at its zenith. There was a Celtic consciousness in sport, theatre, literature, and politics. This consciousness was harnessed as preparations to celebrate the '98 Centenary got under way. Commemorative Brass & Reed bands were formed, books were published, ballads written and sung, cheap prints of patriots were proudly displayed. Subscription lists were opened to raise money to commemorate what was seen as the 'glory' of the people's rebellion. Throughout the south-east of Ireland, particularly in the counties of Wicklow and Wexford, monuments to the insurrection of 1798 abound. Every town, many villages and even cross-roads are decorated with reminders of that bloody summer. Some bear an inscription recalling a battle or skirmish or evil deed. Many of these, particularly in the towns and larger villages, are topped by the strapping figure of a pikeman. These statues have several major features in common. They stand erect, proud, defiant. Broad shoulders are held back, deep chests pushed forward, muscular torsos tapering to narrow waists. The forearms are sinewy and strong. The hands resolutely grip the smooth, perfectly straight shafts of pikes, the heads of which are masterpieces of the blacksmith's craft. The hair is wavy and brushed back from strong, clean faces. In short, they exude nobility. Their bearing, their purpose, their sacrifice is the stuff of untainted virtue. To paraphrase the film-director John Ford, "when the legend is better than the fact, cast the legend".

The monument in Wicklow town is typical of these statues. The handsome, clean-cut young figure is, we are told, a likeness of William Byrne - better known as Billy Byrne of Ballymanus - and, by all accounts, it is a remarkable likeness. He was twenty-three at the time of the rebellion. His physique, good looks, and camaraderie singled him out. If he had not become embroiled in the rising, there could, in all probability, have been songs and stories about him anyway. Likewise, had he been five-foot-two and suffering from rickets his role in the rebellion would not have become enshrined in the folk memory the way that it did.

How could such raw material be allowed to go untapped? Quite simply, it couldn't, with the result that Billy Byrne was immortalised. Anecdotes, which tread the narrow path between truth and wishful-thinking, have been used by his supporters and his detractors to strengthen their particular versions of his role in '98. For two hundred years, the descendants of those factions have perpetuated and embellished the tales. Billy was the epitome of selfless heroism; Byrne was the traitor who turned from yeoman to rebel, only to prove useless to his companions at Vinegar Hill where they accused him of cowardice in battle. Billy was the dashing commander of the Wicklow United Irishmen; Byrne was caught up in the rebellion against his wishes. Take your pick.

Shortly after his trial in 1799, an edited version of the transcript was published in Dublin. Researchers have used that transcript as a primary source in piecing together various aspects of the Wexford/Wicklow rebellion. Now, for the first time in almost two hundred years, that transcript is re-issued to give a wider readership an opportunity to judge for themselves the part played by Billy Byrne of Ballymanus.

*Jim Rees, 1996*

# Billy Byrne of Ballymanus

Come, all you loyal heroes, I pray you'll lend an ear,
And listen to these verses I'm going to declare,
Concerning Billy Byrne, of fame and high renown,
Who was tried and hanged in Wicklow as a traitor to the crown.

In the year of '98, brave boys, we got reason to complain,
We lost our chief commander, Billy Byrne was his name.
In Dublin he was taken and brought to Wicklow gaol,
And to our great misfortune, for him they'd take no bail.

When he was taken prisoner, the traitors all came in.
There was Dixon, Doyle, Toole, Davis, and likewise Bid Doolin.
They thought it little scruple his precious blood to spill
And deprive the County Wicklow of the flower of Pleasant-hill.

Now that they had him taken, they home against him swore
That he upon Mount Pleasant a captain's title bore,
And the king's grand army before his men he did review
And with one piece of cannon marched on to Carrigrue.

It would melt your heart with pity how the traitors all agreed,
That at his father's table so frequently did feed
And in his brother's kitchen where many did him see,
Sure the Byrnes were well rewarded for their hospitality.

It would make your heart to bleed how the traitor did explain,
He swore Byrne worked the cannon on Arklow's bloody plain.
He swore he worked the cannon, that the pikemen he did drill,
And on his retreat to Gorey three loyalists did he kill.

My curse on you, Mat Davis, I will not curse your soul.
It was at the bench of Wicklow you swore without control.
You thought it little scruple his precious blood to spill,
That never robbed, nor burned, nor any man did kill.

Where are the odious traitors - why onward don't they come
To prosecute those prisoners that now are in Rathdrum?
The devil has them fast in chains, repenting for their sins
In lakes of fire and brimestone, and sulphur to their chins.

When the devil saw them coming he sang a pleasant song,
Saying "You're welcome, Mathew Davis. What kept you so long?
Where is the traitor Dixon, to the crown so loyal and true?
Sure I have a warm corner for cursed Bid Doolin too".

Success to Billy Byrne, may his fame forever shine,
Through Holland, France and Flanders, and all along the Rhine.
May the Lord have mercy on him, and all such men as he,
That stand upright for Ireland's cause, and die for liberty.

# CONTENTS

# THE
# TRYAL
## OF

# WILLIAM BYRNE

of Ballymanus, County of Wicklow, Esq.

On charges of being a Principal Leader in the late rebellion, and concerned in several murders in the same; held before

A Military Tribunal at Wicklow,

*BY ORDER OF*

## Major General Eustace,

On Monday the 24th of June and Continued by Adjournment to the 2nd of July 1799, with the Prisoner's Defence, the Judgement of the Court - Sentence, &c, with his Excellency the Lord Lieutenant's decision thereon.

To which is added a Copy of a Memorial on behalf of the Prisoner, laid before his Excellency, and by him transmitted to the Commanding Officer at Wicklow for his report together with his Answer thereto.

-------------------------------

# PROCEEDINGS, &c., &c.

## PRESIDENT
### *John King, Major, Fermanagh Militia*

MEMBERS:
Captain Leslie, Fermanagh Militia.
Captain King, Rathdrum Cavalry
Lt. Cabbott, Fermanagh Militia.
Captain Carroll, Wicklow Cavalry.
Lt. Winslow, Fermanagh Militia.
Lt. E. Armstrong, Fermanagh Militia.


## THE CHARGES

William Byrne charged that he being enrolled as a Yeoman in the Wicklow Yeoman Cavalry, and as such, having taken the oath of allegiance prescribed for yeomen, afterwards became a rebel, and joined the rebel army, then in arms against the King and Government of Ireland.
-      that he was instrumental in calling, and influencing into rebellion divers of His Majesty's subjects
-      that he was a Captain or principal leader in  said rebel army
-      the said William Byrne is also charged with being concerned and an accessary in the murder of Isaac Langrell in Gorey, in the month of June, 1798, and also with being concerned in the murder of three other persons at the rebel camp at Mount Pleasant, whose names are unknown.


*June 24th, 1799:*   Thomas Hugo, Esq. sworn

Witness deposes that he was Lieutenant in the Yeoman Wicklow Cavalry, and the prisoner William Byrne was admitted and enrolled a member of that corps;  and as witness heard and believes, took the oath prescribed for yeomen.  That prisoner continued upwards of six

2

months in said corps, and was then expelled, in consequence of his refusing to take a test oath, purporting, that the deponent never was, and never would be a United Irishman, and that such oath was taken freely and voluntarily, which oath was taken by the whole corps except the prisoner and four others who were expelled.

*Question by Prisoner:* Did I not, during the six months I continued in that corps, obey all orders which had been given me?
A.  You did.
Q.  Did I not, during that period, conduct myself as a soldier and a loyal man?
A.  You did for any thing I know.
Q.  Was any regulation in the troop to take place until a week after it's being proposed?
A.  With respect to the ballotting for members it was so, but I do not know it was so upon any other occasion.
Q.  Were there any other members expelled at the same time?
A.  There were four others expelled at the same time for not taking the test.
Q.  Had the rebellion commenced, or were there any rebels in arms at the time I was expelled?
A.  I knew of none.
Q.  Did you not consider my expulsion as a punishment for not having taken the oath?
A.  I did.

*By the Court:*
Q.  Was it merely as a punishment he was expelled, or was it because he was considered an improper person to be continued in the loyal yeomanry corps?
A.  It was on account of his suspected disloyalty in having refused the test oath.

*By the Prisoner:*
Q.  Have you heard any of the corps previous to my expulsion declare or advise that I should be expelled for disloyalty?
A.  I did.
Q.  Was not my refusal to take the proposed oath the principal reason assigned for my expulsion?

A.  It was.

Q.  Do you not therefore think that my having ceased to be a yeoman was involuntary on my part and no desertion?

A.  You were turned out.

*By the Court:*

Q.  Did you hear and believe that when the test oath was first proposed to the prisoner, he requested of Captain Carroll, the commander of the corps, a few days to consider, and that at the end of those days, prisoner being again called upon, absolutely refused to take the test, and was therefore instantly expelled?

A.  I did hear it and do believe it.

*By the Prisoner:*

Q.  Do you conceive that a yeoman expelled from his corps can be considered a deserter from that corps?

A.  I do not.

Q.  After I was expelled, was I considered a deserter?

A.  I never did.

*By the Court:*

Q.  Did you consider the prisoner a deserter from the cause of loyalty?

A.  I did.

Q.  Do you not conceive that the meaning of the word deserter, applied to a military man, means flying from the corps or regiment to which he belongs?

A.  I do.

*By the Prisoner:*

Q.  Have you ever heard, or do you believe, that I was at any time, after my ceasing to be a member of your corps, a yeoman in any other yeomanry corps?

A.  I never did hear it, nor do I believe it.

Q.  Were any of those who were expelled at the same time, and for the same cause with me, afterwards admitted into your corps?

A.  One of the name of Freeman was proposed by me, and admitted.

4

*By the Court:*
Q.   Why did you propose Freeman and not the others expelled?
A.   Because it appeared that Freeman's conduct in refusing the test had been influenced by some of those expelled and he solicited to be re-admitted upon his taking the test, which accordingly he did take, and none of the others expelled ever made any application to be re-admitted.

*By the Prisoner:*
A certificate signed W.H. Hume, dated 13th May, 1799, purporting that the prisoner, in the middle of May 1798, had applied to be admitted into his corps but, there being no vacancy, was not admitted - (produced to Mr. Hugo, which Mr. Hugo believes is the handwriting of Mr. Hume, and from that certificate witness believes prisoner did make such application).
Q.   Do you believe that I was a yeoman at the time I applied to Captain Hume to be admitted a member of his corps?
A.   I do not.

*By The Court*
Q.   Is it not more criminal in a man to become a rebel leader after having as a yeoman taken the oath prescribed by law than in one who had not been a yeoman or taken such an oath?

*Objection by the Prisoner:*
Because it is a matter of opinion, and not applicable to the charge asked on the part of the prosecution of the witness, called on behalf of the crown.

*By the Court:*   Over-ruled and witness called to answer.
A.   I think it is.

*June 25th, 1799:*

Prisoner admits that he was enrolled as a yeoman in the Wicklow cavalry, and took the oath prescribed for yeomen; continued in that corps six months and was then expelled for refusing to take the test oath.

5

# Bridget Doolin sworn

Knows and identifies the prisoner: Witness was at the rebel camp at Gorey Hill before the battle of Arklow, when the prisoner at the head of about 300 men marched into camp; he rode with a drawn sword in his hand; the party he headed were called the Ballymanus corps, and were armed some with guns and some with pikes.

- that the prisoner was called Captain and acted as such.

- that the prisoner marched his men to the attack of Arklow, with the rebel army, where he also acted as Captain. When the prisoner and his party approached Gorey Hill, he was met by the music of the camp, consisting of drums, fifes, fiddles and bag-pipes; and rejoicing was made upon the occasion. After the defeat of the rebels at Arklow, they marched back to Gorey Hill and soon after news was brought into the camp that one Langrell, an Orange-man, was taken in Gorey. A party was thereupon ordered to the town, under the command of the prisoner.

- that witness was asked to go and see an Orange-man piked, and she went to Gorey churchyard for that purpose, where she saw Isaac Langrell lying on the ground with signs of life in him, he having being piked before she arrived, and before he expired, a man with a hay-knife set in a stick struck the said Langrell across the neck, which nearly severed the head from the body.

- that the prisoner William Byrne was present and appeared to have the command of the party that put Langrell to death; and upon the stroke of the hay-knife being given, the prisoner William Byrne said to his party, "March off, for the heretic will rise no more". The prisoner, who had a sword in his hand, marched away with the party.

- that the rebel army marched from Gorey Hill to Limerick Hill, from whence one part marched to Mount Pleasant, and the other party to Carnew; witness went to Carnew, prisoner went with the party to Mount Pleasant, both parties met afterwards at Kilcavan, where she saw the prisoner calling out his men into ranks.

- the rebel army afterwards marched to Carrigrua, and from thence to Vinegar Hill, where she again saw the prisoner acting as commander of the Ballymanus corps

6

- that said corps was ordered into the town of Enniscorthy, whereupon some objections were made by the corps against going there, some saying they would not march without being led by Garret Byrne, and others saying they would not go without their Captain William Byrne, the prisoner.

- that upon this occasion another commander of the rebels charged the prisoner William Byrne with cowardice and prisoner replied he was as stout as him, and would exchange a shot with him. The rebel army was very soon after dispersed by the King's army, and witness never saw prisoner since until this day in court.

*Cross-examined by Prisoner:*

Q. Where were you born and what is your age?

A. I was born in Carnew and am under 20 years of age.

Q. In what manner, before joining the rebels, did you earn your livelihood?

A. I was a servant.

Q. In whose service did you live, and how long immediately before you joined the rebels?

A. I lived with Mr. M'Cormick, in Carnew, but was not in service for half a year before I joined the rebels.

Q. How did you support yourself the half-year you were not in service?

A. I lived with my father in Carnew.

Q. At what time did you join the rebels?

A. I joined the rebels immediately after Colonel Walpole's death, and before the Battle of Arklow.

Q. And what was the reason you joined them?

A. Because we thought we would have had the day.

Q. How long did you remain with the rebels, and how did you support yourself?

A. From the battle of Gorey, until the rebels went to the Boyne. I supported myself by taking provisions wherever I could get them and sometimes the men gave me share of what they got.

Q. Where do you now live and how long have you continued in your present residence?

A. In Rathdrum, and I have continued in Rathdrum half a year.

Q. Are you at liberty or in confinement in your present residence?

A. I am in confinement.

Q.  In whose custody are you in, in Rathdrum, and by whose order?

A.  In the custody of Philips, a constable, by order of Mr. Wainwright.

Q.  When, and for what reason, were you taken into custody?

A.  About nine months ago, I was first taken because I had been out with the rebels.

Q.  Where were you when you were taken prisoner?

A.  At Coolkenno.

Q.  How are you at present supported and furnished with clothes?

A.  By order of two magistrates.

Q.  Have you ever before been a witness on any, and what, trials by court martial?

A.  I have been a witness at Rathdrum on trials of rebels.

Q.  Did you not, at a court-martial held at Rathdrum, swear against prisoners who were acquitted?

A.  I did and the prisoners were acquitted and what I then swore there was the truth.

Q.  Did you not with your own hands set fire to baggage cars belonging to his majesty?

A.  The rebels pulled the furze and I set fire to them.

Q.  Have you ever declared that you were determined to swear away the life of William Byrne, and did you ever declare you could not get your liberty without swearing against him?

A.  I never did say any such word - why should I swear his life away any more than any other man?

Q.  Did you ever speak of the prisoner in the shop of Mr. Manning in Rathdrum, and what did you say of him there?

A.  I was asked was I to go on Billy Byrne's trial, I answered I was, and that was all I said.

Q.  To whom did you mention, in William Manning's shop, what you have now said?

A.  I do not know to whom I mentioned those words, nor do I recollect that any of the family of Manning except the clerk were in the shop at that time, and to my knowledge I never at any time had any conversation respecting the prisoner at Manning's but once.

Q.  Have you ever fought against his majesty's army, and which do you think rebellion or perjury the greater crime?  Do you not conceive it to be a lighter crime in a girl of 18 to swear falsely than to chose to go to the murder of an Orangeman?

*By the Court:*
It is the opinion of this court that the two last questions should not be put as they seem to refer to the oath of secrecy, or United Irishman's oath which 'tis probable the witness took.

*By the Prisoner:*
Q. When you were with the rebels, were there any officers appointed, and how were they generally chosen?
A. I do not know of any officers being appointed but I understood that there were two officers and a captain to every corps.
Q. Had the officers any mark or badge to distinguish them from the common men?
A. There were badges - some wore green spencers - some wore sashes, and some wore skins on their hats.

*By the Court:*
Q. Had the different corps different colours?
A. Most of them had. Ballymanus corps had colours, but I cannot particularly describe them, the prisoner had no distinguishing badge, but he wore a white sword.

*By the Prisoner*
Q. Do you believe that every man, who was appointed a rebel officer, was a sworn United Irishman, and publicly known to be such?
A. As far as I know I believe they were sworn, and I was present when a Captain was sworn.
Q. When and where did you see any oath tendered to a Captain of rebels, and what was the nature of such oath?
A. I saw a Captain sworn at Tombreen at the beginning of this business about a year and a half ago, and that it was a United Irishman's oath which was brought forward by Johnny Toole, a head rebel.
Q. Were there other persons present, and how many when the oath you now mention was tendered, was it usual to swear United Irishmen in the presence of women?
A. There were about 30 present, and women were sworn as well as men.

9

Q.   Do you consider your confinement in Rathdrum a protection or a restraint on your liberty?

A.   Both.

Q.   Do you know or believe, that for some time before the rebellion, the Captains of rebels were busy in assembling and disciplining the men under their command?

A.   They were busy at night and I was present at some of those meetings.

Q.   Have you heard or do you believe that there were more than one Captain to each rebel corps, and was not such Captain elected at a considerable time before the rebellion?

A.   To the corps I knew there was but one Captain, and they were elected a considerable time before the rebellion.

Q.   Was there more than one body of men in the rebel camp known by the name of the Ballymanus corps?

A.   Not that I know of.

Q.   How many days before the battle of Arklow, as you recollect, did the Ballymanus corps come to the camp at Gorey?

A.   As well as I recollect, it was the day before.

Q.   About what time in the day?

A.   As well as I recollect, it was between 12 and one.

Q.   Did you immediately, on the Ballymanus corps coming into the camp, see the prisoner riding before that corps, and hear him called Captain?

A.   I did see him ride before the corps and saw him saluted as Captain.

Q.   Were the different corps of rebels the day before the battle of Arklow, drawn up in military array, and commanded by their Captains?

A.   They were drawn up (and) commanded by their Captains.

Q.   Was the Ballymanus corps drawn up with the rest and at what hour?

A.   Not long after the Ballymanus corps came, in about an hour every corps marched in regular order around a large field at Gorey Hill and the Ballymanus corps marched first.

Q.   Did you see the Captains of the different rebel corps exercise their men on the evening previous to the battle of Arklow?

A. The different corps were drawn up, the gunmen in front, and the pikemen in the rear, and they were marched about, but did not see any other exercise at Gorey Hill.

Q. Were you present at Vinegar Hill at the dispute at the Ballymanus corps, whether they should be commanded by William Byrne or Garret Byrne?

A. I was near enough to hear the words pass.

Q. Was Garret Byrne on Vinegar Hill at that time?

A. He was.

Q. Do you believe that it was from malice to protestants that William Byrne said: "the heretic will rise no more"; and do you believe, that while he was with the rebels, that he would rather have murdered than saved the life of a Protestant?

A. I believe it was from malice or else he would not have made such a speech, and I believe he would rather murder than save a protestant.

*By the Court*

Q. Did it appear to you that William Byrne, the prisoner, if he had been inclined, could have saved the life of Langrell?

A. I am sure that he could, or any man that had such a command.

Q. At what places did you see Garret Byrne between the battle of Arklow and the battle of Vinegar Hill?

A. I saw him at Carrigrua, at Gorey and Vinegar Hill.

Q. Did you hear Leeson examined yesterday?

A. I did not.

Q. On what day, and at what time of the day, was Langrell killed?

A. I cannot recollect the day, but it was about dinner time.

Captain King, a member of the Court, says he was present when Bridget Doolin was examined before the court martial at Rathdrum, and that the prisoners there tried were acquitted, as coming under the Amnesty Act, and not upon any doubt of Bridget Doolin's testimony.

# John Conyers sworn

Witness was taken prisoner the day after the battle of Clough, and carried to the rebel guard-house in Gorey, where he was confined until the morning of the battle of Arklow

- that one Mernagh, a rebel, made interest with the commanders to liberate the witness
- that Perry, Redmond and prisoner, were the three principal commanders
- at the intercession of Mernagh he received a protection drawn up by Redmond and signed by him P. Redmond; it was also signed W.Byrne in witness's presence, by the prisoner, in which protection it was specified, that witness could not under pain of death quit Gorey, but as he was handy in the surgical line, he should stay there to dress wounded men
- that before the march to Arklow, he saw Perry, prisoner and Redmond, as the three principal commanders, making musters of the rebel army, from which he understood amounted to 31,000 men; and heard the prisoner called for to head his party.

*Cross-examined by Prisoner*

Q.  Have you heard or do you know in what manner the captains in the rebel army were appointed or chosen?

A.  I do not.

Q.  Do you not believe that all the captains of rebels had been appointed long before the rebellion, and that they were all sworn United Irishmen, and that they had long been employed in disciplining their men?

A.  I really believe they were, but know nothing except by hear-say.

Q.  Did the signature to the protection signed by the prisoner express that it was given by him as a captain?

A.  It did not.

Q.  Do you not think it probable that the prisoner, from his rank in life, might have influence among the rebels, even if he had no command?

A.  I believe that he had great influence over the rebels as they frequently called to him; and believe he might have influence even if he had no command, as three men who had no command at Vinegar Hill saved my life when I was ordered to be piked.

*By the Court*
Q. You said the rebels frequently called upon prisoner; how or upon what occasions was he so called?
A. The different corps were often called over and when Ballymanus corps was called the prisoner was called upon to head his corps.

*By the Prisoner*
Q. Do you not believe that the prisoner's eldest brother was usually called Mr. Byrne of Ballymanus?
A. I never knew, or to my knowledge, saw prisoner's eldest brother; but I am positive as to the identity of prisoner being one of the person's who signed the protection.
Q. Are you certain that the three Arklow yeomen were in the guard-house at the time of your getting the protection as that the prisoner signed it?
A. I am positive prisoner signed the protection, but am not so positive that the three Arklow yeomen were at that time in the guard-house, but believe they were.

*June 26th:*　　　Thomas Dowse sworn

Knows the prisoner. On the 15th of June 1798, witness was taken prisoner by the rebels and taken to the rebel camp at Limerick Hill near Gorey:
- that he there saw the prisoner, with whom he had been intimate, and applied to him, supposing him to have influence to restore a considerable quantity of witness's effects, which was then brought to the camp on car
- Prisoner said, "come, come, the effects must go down to Limerick", where they were taken and never restored to witness.
- On the 17th of June the rebel army marched to Mount Pleasant, whither witness was taken, and, soon after, three men and two boys were brought in as prisoners, and heard three shots near the carriage

13

in which witness was detained (and) by which witness understood the three men were killed

- that the rebels were attacked by a party of the king's army which, after the firing of some cannon by the rebels, retreated
- the town of Tinnehaly near Mount Pleasant was burned, and after the town was set on fire, and while it continued burning, one Father Toole, a Popish Priest, celebrated Mass to the rebel army, then in sight of the burning town
- that the rebel army, in the night of the 17th, marched to Kilcavan Hill, where they arrived early on the morning of the 18th
- that about the hour of three in the afternoon, the King's army appeared and fired some shells at the rebel army, but did not come to close attack during the firing of the artillery. He saw the prisoner riding about and prisoner got a fall from his horse, by which his arm was hurted, which he afterwards carried in a sling, as he believes
- about nightfall of the 18th, after the King's army had withdrawn, a meeting was held apart from the common men, by Kyan, Perry, Fitzgerald, Mernagh, Redmond and Prisoner, and some others which persons witness understood were leading men in the rebel army, and that the meeting was held for the purpose of consulting what course they should take, or what should be done
- witness was at the distance of ten or twelve yards and within view of the meeting, but he did not hear anything which passed
- that Perry wore a uniform, which witness believes he had when he was a yeoman, Kyan nor prisoner had no distinguishing badge, and believes Kyan, Perry and Fitzgerald, had more authority than the prisoner
- that in the night of the 18th the rebel army marched to Camolin, and on the morning of the 19th, witness saw Kyan and prisoner in a post-chaise, Kyan soon after called to witness and told him he could not preserve the witness's life any longer, and believes he would have been killed at Camolin, had it not been for the prisoner's interference.
- that witness soon after effected his escape
- there were at least ten Priests at Limerick Hill
- one Roger Pierce, a Loyalist, was brought by some rebels into Limerick, and there put to death, in a most barbarous and inhuman manner

- that he did and does still believe the prisoner had a command in the rebel army and no common man could have influence to save the witness's life as he believes the prisoner did

- that during his continuance with the rebels, it was the practice with the common men every morning to chalk on their hats 'J.H.S.' and those who had not hats had those letters chalked on some part of their clothing.

*Cross-examined by Prisoner*

Q. When you applied to the prisoner to interfer on your behalf for your goods, did you not conceive that his rank in life would have influence among the common people, and do you not think that one of his family would have influence among the lower class of people, although such person had no command?

A. To my belief he had a command, as I said before, and that he would from his family have had influence among the lower class of people.

Q. When you first applied to the prisoner had you any other reason than his rank in life for believing that he had a command in the rebel army?

A. I did believe at that time that from his rank in life he had a command, but had then no other reason for believing so, but by what passed at Kilcavan Hill, as before stated, I had afterwards other reasons for believing he had a command.

Q. Do you not believe that the prisoner would, while you were with the rebels, have been willing to do you an act of kindness in his power?

A. I am sure he was willing.

Q. Do you not believe that if the prisoner had command, and had without permission restored you your goods, he would have suffered punishment if he had no command?

A. I believe he would, but I believe he would not if he had a command.

Q. Do you recollect the prisoner having said to you: "You need not fear as far as I can serve you, but you must apply to Kyan, or some other person having a command to get you your goods", or words to that effect?

A. I do verily believe he did.

Q. Did the prisoner give any order to have the goods taken down to Limerick?

A. He did not, that I heard the cars were going on.

Q. Can you take it upon you to swear, that some of those who consulted at Kilcavan, might not have been men without command in the rebel army?

A. Some of them might, for anything I know to the contrary, but I believe everyone of them had more or less command.

Q. Was Barny Murray, whom you have mentioned, a rebel Captain or commander?

A. I verily believe Murray was surgeon or doctor to the rebel army.

A. Do you not believe that all the rebel Captains had an equal command in their army?

A. I do not believe they had for some could do more than others.

A. Might not the prisoner, although without command, have been called upon by the leaders of the rebels to advise the best line of march, or on any other subject, on account of his knowledge of the country, or for some other reason?

A. I do not believe it, it might be possible but not probable, for he must have had some command.

Q. Were those who you saw mounted in the rebel army confined to a particular part of the army or did they not ride at large along the ranks?

A. I saw, as I believe, twenty privates for one officer riding along the ranks of infantry, as the men who had horses were not confined to any particular part of the army.

Q. Do you not think it probable that if each rebel corps had but one Captain, the duty and situation of such officer would oblige him to remain with his men and to have them under his immediate inspection?

A. I do not know but there might have been five Captains to each corps, but if there was but one Captain he no doubt would have more to do - and I believe the Captains did often leave their corps to the command of inferior officers, for I believe they were not under good jurisdiction.

Q. Was the prisoner, to the best of your knowledge, a relation of Kyan, and do you not think it probable that if the prisoner was in ill-health Kyan would (although Prisoner had no command) have permitted the prisoner to travel in his carriage?

A. The prisoner, to the best of my knowledge, is not a relation of Kyan, but supposing he was a relation would, in case of his (the prisoner's) illness and although he might not have had a command, have taken him into the carriage, which carriage was the property of Mr. White of Rockingham and brought by a rebel party to Mount Pleasant, and I also believe that if Prisoner was not a relation and had no command Kyan would not have taken him into the carriage.

Q. You have said you don't know whether the prisoner was present at Pierce's murder, from what you know of the prisoner, do you think him capable of countenancing so barbarous an act?

A. I do not believe him capable of so barbarous an act, but am certain the prisoner was in the rebel camp that day.

Q. Are you a Protestant, and do you think it credible that prisoner would massacre a Protestant as an Heretic, or do you think it more probable that he would exert himself to save the life of a Protestant than assist in his murder?

A. I cannot answer for the heart of man.

Q. About what time of day was Pierce murdered?

A. Between the hours of two and three.

Q. Do you not believe that the three men who were shot at Mount Pleasant suffered under the orders of those who had the chief command of the rebel army at that time?

A. I cannot tell.

*By the Court*

Q. Do you think that when the prisoner met in consultation at Kilcavan Hill, that if he had been consulted merely for information respecting his knowledge of the country, that he would, if he had no command, been permitted to remain to hear the result of the consultation?

A. Prisoner remained with the other leaders until the whole broke up, and I believe he would not have been permitted to remain to hear the result had he not been a leader and in the plot.

Q. At about what time of day were the three men killed in Mount Pleasant?

A. In the evening about four or five o'clock, it was after the army appeared and went into Tinnehaly.

17

# William Poole sworn

He was a prisoner in the rebel guard-house at Gorey about the 14th of June 1798, he applied to Captain Redmond, a rebel leader, for his liberty and a protection. Redmond gave him a protection signed by himself, of the import following: "permit the bearer William Poole to go home to his place unmolested as we have two sons of his as hostages".

The guard placed over witness refused to obey Redmond's protection unless it was signed by the prisoner William Byrne, the prisoner soon after came into the guard-house and, witness having applied to him, he immediately signed the protection or pass which witness had received from Redmond, without expressing that he was a Captain or any other officer. Witness remaining in the guard-house, until next morning and was then permitted to go out to Gorey.

# Benjamin Warren sworn

Knows the prisoner. The day after the battle of Arklow, witness was a prisoner in the guard-house of Gorey with other loyalists.

- That the prisoner, William Byrne, came into the guard-house in a violent manner and asked why the Orange-men were suffered to remain there, and said he would take their lives and drew his sword, with which he made a blow at witness's neck, which witness perceiving stooped his head and received a cut on it, a little above his ear, witness was taken to the rebel infirmary where he was told by Mr. White, a regular bred surgeon whom the rebels obliged to act for them, that his skull was fractured and witness was told the cut was five inches in length, witness remained about two months very ill in consequence of said wound and betimes it is yet sore and fiery. A Captain Moncks came into the guard-house immediately upon the witness being struck by the prisoner and said to prisoner that he was a cowardly rascal for striking his prisoner and that he would have him broke of his commission, and Moncks presented a pistol to prisoner's breast and threatened to shoot him if he did not drop his sword. Prisoner did drop his sword and begged witness's pardon at the desire of Moncks.

*Cross-examined by Prisoner*

Q. Was Moncks, whom you have mentioned, usually called Captain?

A. He was in my hearing.

Q. Did you know or hear any other person called Captain among the rebels?

A. No one but Perry.

Q. At what time of the day did this transaction happen?

A. I believe about ten or eleven.

Q. In what room in the guard-house did this happen, and who were present?

A. It was in the large room, and Patchel, Farmer, and some others were present.

Q. Is Dr. White, who dressed your head, living or dead, and if living where is he?

A. He was living in Donaghmore in the county of Wexford when I left home.


# James Patchel sworn

Knows the prisoner. Witness was a prisoner in the rebel guard-house the day after the battle of Arklow, was present when the prisoner came in and said: "Why are those bloody Orange fellows kept here? I have by this day lost by them many of my friends", and Patchel minutely corroborates the testimony of Benjamin Warren. While witness was a prisoner at Gorey, he saw the prisoner at the head of the Ballymanus corps, which appeared to consist of about two or 300 men, march up and down the town several times, the men crying out "Ballymanus, Ballymanus", the prisoner when at the head of the corps had a drawn sword in his hand. Moncks was Captain of the guard, by whose division witness was taken, and he claimed witness as his prisoner.

Q. When the prisoner came into the guard-house of Gorey, could you definitely hear the conversation between Moncks and him?

A. I did definitely hear what I have related as having passed between Moncks and prisoner.

Q. If Moncks had at the same time said anything more to prisoner, could you have heard that also?

A. I could have heard him but he did not say any more.

Q. Were not the prisoners who were in the guard-house of Gorey closely watched by the rebels who were on guard?

A. They were.

# John Walker sworn

Witness was taken prisoner by the rebels and taken to Gorey Hill previous to the battle of Arklow, and witness to save his life consented to carry a pike. Saw the prisoner William Byrne march from Gorey to the battle of Arklow at the head of the Ballymanus corps, he rode and was armed with a large crooked sword, he first saw the prisoner lead on his men at Arklow and when they were beat back he returned and brought them up again and did so several times and in particular one time the Priest Murphy, in order to induce the men to return to battle, took out and shook his handkerchief, and declared he would shake off the Orange-men's balls. In consequence of this, the prisoner did bring up some of his men, others ran away, the prisoner was called Captain, and (witness) believes the Ballymanus corps consisted of between two and 300 men, of which the prisoner appeared to have the chief command. Witness saw no other commander of that corps, he saw the prisoner at the head of his corps on the Arklow road, at the turn to Polahoney, where several rebels were killed and wounded by the King's artillery. The prisoner was shot through the hat.

After the battle of Arklow, witness was taken prisoner to Gorey, and being a blacksmith resident at Mt. Nebo, about three miles distant, he was sent there under a guard to shoe rebel horses and continued there until the army marched to Mount Pleasant. That while at home he heard two men, Langrell and Wheatly, who had been taken prisoners by the rebels, had been piked to death in the church yard of Gorey.

At Mount Pleasant, he saw the prisoner have, and exercise, a command over the Ballymanus corps, and had the same command at Kilcavan, where prisoner had his hand tied up in consequence of a fall from his horse, and heard the rebels lament that Captain Byrne had been hurted. Witness had a brother taken prisoner by the rebels, and shot, and piked by them on Gorey Hill. From Kilcavan the rebels marched by Carrigrua to Vinegar Hill, but witness did not see prisoner after he left Kilcavan.

*Cross-examined by Prisoner*

Q. In what part of the rebel army was Captain Murphy of Monaseed's corps, which you have joined, posted during the battle of Arklow and were you on horse-back?

A. I did not ride. There was no regularity in the corps at Arklow; they were frequently called together by their Captains, by the name of the corps.

Q. How many rebels were engaged at the battle of Arklow, as you believe?

A. There were a great many, but cannot tell how many.

Q. Was Murphy's corps engaged in the battle of Arklow, and how long?

A. It was engaged and when any of the men dropped the others ran away.

Q. During the heat and confusion of battle, were you not much alarmed for your own safety?

A. I was, and kept along the dyke of a ditch.

Q. Could you undertake to prove every circumstance that happened to all the rebel leaders at the battle of Arklow?

A. I could not, but I saw my own Captain Murphy engaged, and some other leaders, but do not know who they were.

Witness was taken prisoner by the rebels and brought to their camp at Mount Pleasant where he saw the prisoner, who was called Captain Byrne of the Ballymanus corps.

- One Joshua Chase, a loyalist, an old man, was likewise a prisoner and guarded by one Mergin or Bergin, who was called and acted as sergeant of the guard. Mergin had Chase on the ground, whose arms were tied close and said he would cut Chase's head off. The prisoner, William Byrne, happened to come to the place and seeing what Mergin was going to do, drew his sword and said he would cut Mergin's head off if he hurted the prisoner Chase; and ordered Mergin, as being drunk and unfit to have the care of the guard, to be removed and another person to take his place, and accordingly Mergin was removed and one Kavanagh took charge of the prisoners. The prisoner, William Byrne, released one William Lewis, who was also a prisoner, and upon Lewis's asking him for a protection, prisoner said "let me see the man that dare say anything to you". Lewis then departed without interruption. Witness in order to save his life, consented to join the rebels and a pike was given him. Witness saw the prisoner mounted both at Mount Pleasant and Kilcavan, armed with a sword, riding amongst the rebel forces. The reason why the witness was afraid of being killed at that time was that three men of the name of Free, Foster and Berry, who were loyalists, were shot in the camp very near witness and he expected to meet the same fate. Witness heard that Free and Foster were killed in revenge for a rebel who had been killed by the King's army that morning near the camp, and Berry was killed for being an Orangeman. Chase and one Redmond, being old men, and two small boys, were that day set at liberty by order of Captain Perry, who asked was there any charge against them, but no charge was made.

*Cross-examined by Prisoner*
Q. You say Mergin was a sergeant; do you not believe that in the rebel army there were several ranks of officers between private and captain?
A. I never heard there were.

Q.   Had not the rebel officers some distinguishing badge, and were they not much better dressed than the common men?

A.   They had.  I saw one man, Carroll, who was called Captain, wear a green spencer, with an officer hat with a brush over it and a black cockade and a green one over it; and those who were named officers were better dressed and had nicer arms than the common men.  Some officers had not a distinguishing badge except that they were better clothed.

Q.   Had the prisoner anything in his dress at Mount Pleasant to distinguish him from the common men?

A.   Prisoner wore an outside great coat, a caroline hat, boots and spurs and well mounted with a very nice sword, which he carried drawn in his hand, which was not usually done by the common men.

Q.   From the interference of prisoner in behalf of Lewis, do you not believe he would, as far as in him lay, rather assist in saving a protestant prisoner than join in his murder?

A.   I do not think he would, I think he would rather go against him than save him.

Q.   Did you not at Mount Pleasant see many men who were not rebel Captains ride and wear boots and spurs, and did you not see some man or men with swords who were not rebel Captains?

A.   I did not see any man or men at Mount Pleasant who had swords, except Mergin who was not considered a rebel Captain.  I did see several men ride, but never saw one but an officer have boots and spurs, nor did I ever see any but an officer ride about the camp with a drawn sword.

Q.   From the carriages and marquees of Kyan and Perry being in the quarter where the three men were shot, do you not believe they had the principal command in that quarter?

A.   I believe they had.


*By the Court*

Q.   While you were with the rebels did you ever see the sergeant or officer of the guard changed but by the command of a superior officer?

A.   I did not.  I saw the guard changed at Limerick guard-house, by order of one Mernagh, who was deemed a Captain, and at Mount Pleasant as before stated.

# Joshua Chase sworn

Witness is a feeble old man in the 80th year of his age, he was taken prisoner in Tinnehaly in the night of the 16th of June, and carried to the camp at Mount Pleasant, and guarded with several other loyalist prisoners by a large party of pikemen, among whom was one Mergen who witness understood was sergeant of the guard. On the 17th, Mergen charged witness with being an Orange-man and a maker of Orange-men and having three sons Orange-men, which witness denied. Mergin desired witness to bless himself, he could not, except by saying the Lord bless him: "Then have you any religion?" Witness said he had and that his religion was derived from the scriptures. "No", said Mergin, "your religion is derived from a rogue and a whore", and grossly abused witness and said Henry VIII and Queen Elizabeth were the rogue and the whore; upon which witness replied he had read the scriptures from Genesis to Revelations, and had not seen the name of King Henry VIII or Queen Elizabeth. Mergin then tied witness's arms which he drew backwards by a cord until they were drawn near out of the sockets, whereby witness suffered great pain. Witness was tied by Mergin about the hour of eleven and continued in that situation until about four or five in the evening. Some time after his being so tied, he was ordered by Mergin to go on his knees and then a party of gunmen were called to shoot witness and others called out to pike witness. Some time after he heard a rumour that Captain Byrne was coming and Mr. William Byrne of Ballymanus immediately came up. Witness knew William Byrne of Ballymanus and is positive that he is the man that came up, but witness's sight having since failed him, he cannot now see sufficiently well to say whether the prisoner at the bar be William Byrne of Ballymanus.

Upon Byrne's coming Mergin said to him, "Captain, what shall we do with them?", meaning as witness believes Berry and witness who were lying on the ground tied, which Berry was afterwards in the evening shot. Mr. William Byrne of Ballymanus answered: "I don't care what the devil you do with them, if you don't choose to kill them, put them in the guard-house". William Byrne then passed through the guard and in some short time returned, did not speak to witness, but heard he said some thing to others which witness did not hear. Mergin took witness twice before a person who assumed the character of justice of the peace, and charged witness with being the maker of Orange-men, witness desired the justice to put Mergin on his oath, which the justice declined saying it was sabbathday and he would not administer an oath. Mergin afterwards brought witness back to the guard and said he would not trouble himself to look for witnesses to prove witness was an Orange-man, but would make the matter short, then made witness lie down when he swore he would cut witness's head off and laid the edge of a sword across witness's neck, which he repeated a second time.

Two gentlemen, in some short time after, came riding by, who witness understood were principal commanders. One of them said to witness: "Old man, come here. What fault have you committed?". Witness said he could not tell and requested he would call any honest man in the camp to tell what he had done. Said gentleman then called aloud and desired to know what witness had done and having again called to the same effect and no one appearing, said person, who witness believed was General Perry, ordered witness to be set at liberty, and sent a man to guard him out of the camp. Some short time before the general came by, Mergin said he had had a great deal of trouble bringing in prisoners and if they were set at liberty he would resign his command, and stuck his sword in the ground. He was pressed to keep the command which he refused and went away in a passion. One Kavanagh then took command of the guard. This declaration was made by Mergin soon after William Byrne had passed the second time through the guard. When the rebel party, which consisted principally of horse, came into Tinnehaly, they ordered that such of the inhabitants as were Roman Catholics should put up lights in their houses, none of which were burned but all others were.

*Cross-examined by Prisoner*
Q. Do you know the names of any of the nine prisoners that were in the rebel camp with you; mention them.
A. There were Thomas Paslow, Marks Redmond, William Myers, William Graham, one called one of Gowan's blood-hounds, and Berry who was put to death, John Dagg and a boy of the name of Kinch, and Richard Williams.

Q. About what time of day did you first see William Byrne of Ballymanus in the rebel camp?
A. The day was far spent.


## Thomas Paslow sworn

Witness is in the 89th year of his age, identifies the prisoner. Witness was taken prisoner by the rebels in Tinnehaly on the 17th of June, and as he was led by the market house, which was then in flames, some of the rebels proposed that he should be thrown into the burning house, others opposed that saying "we will soon send him to a hotter place".

Witness was then taken to Mount Pleasant and placed under the guard commanded by Mergin, who acted as sergeant. Chase and other prisoners were there. Witness was several times threatened to be piked for being an Orange-man and heretic. After some time William Byrne, the prisoner, came up and, entering the circle, asked Mergin what occasioned the delay: "Why do you not despatch them?" and after some conversation with Mergin, prisoner William Byrne went away, but soon came again and finding the prisoners were still there, was very angry with the sergeant, and on the sergeant telling the prisoner William Byrne that he (Byrne) had not the command, Byrne called him a rascal and said: "I will let you know the command is in me". Witness was afterwards set at liberty by General Perry, as he heard him called, as being an old man against whom no charge lay. Chase was discharged at the same time.

*Cross-examined by Prisoner*
Q. About what hour on the 17th of June did you see William Byrne at Mount Pleasant?
A. I was taken about nine in the morning and I was confused afterwards. I cannot recollect the hour I saw prisoner.
Q. Did you hear William Byrne use any other expression respecting the prisoners than that which you have mentioned?
A. I did not.
Q. Had not Chase an equal opportunity with you to hear what William Byrne said, respecting the prisoners?

Q.   Chase was confined a length of time before me and he therefore had a better opportunity of hearing more than me.

## William Graham sworn

Witness is now about the age of 14, was taken prisoner by the rebels and brought to Mount Pleasant.   He and other prisoners were guarded by pikemen and Mergin was the sergeant.   The prisoner William Byrne came into the ring with a drawn sword in his hand and was asked by some of them what should be done with the children.   Byrne answered: "Damn them; kill them or do what you like with them", and then Byrne went away.   Some time after, six men came up to try the grown men and then witness and another boy were turned out.

*Cross-examined by Prisoner*
Q.   Were Chase and Paslow present when William Byrne made use of the expressions you have mentioned?
A.   Chase was there, but I do recollect Paslow.
Q.   Did you hear William Byrne use any other expressions respecting the prisoners, and could Paslow and Chase hear what he said?
A.   I did not hear Byrne use any other words.   Chase was lying on the ground and was very near me.
Q.   Were you with the prisoners when William Byrne first came up to them?
A.   I was.
Q.   Was the time when you saw William Byrne come up to the prisoners the first time of his coming to them, as you have heard and believe?
A.   I believe it was.   I left all the other prisoners in custody, except the boy who was liberated with me.

# John Hopkins sworn

Knows the prisoner. He was out with the rebels and after some time was at the camp at Gorey Hill where he saw the prisoner William Byrne march into the camp, at the head of between 2 and 300 men, with a drawn sword in his hand, who were called the Ballymanus corps, and Byrne was called by them their Captain. The rebels in the camp as a mark of their joy at seeing so large a number join them put up their hats on the top of the pikes and huzza'd.

Witness saw the prisoner at the head of the Ballymanus corps march to the battle of Arklow, and as far as the Charter school, but as witness's division was on the other side of the town, he knows nothing more of the prisoner during the battle.

He did not see the prisoner afterwards, (as witness went home for refreshments), until he saw him at Mount Pleasant, and there only for a short time. He saw the prisoner at Kilcavan, at the head of the Ballymanus corps, when the King's army appeared. The rebels then marched to Carrigrua and to Vinegar Hill. Prisoner did not march on the road at the head of his corps, but all the gentlemen, Perry, Kyan, Prisoner, and others, rode in the front of the rebel army, but believes that all that rode so in the front were Captains or officers. Saw prisoner at Vinegar Hill, but witness, being posted down one side of the hill, did not see the prisoner during the battle.

*Cross-examined by Prisoner*

Q. At what time of the day did William Byrne come to Gorey Hill?

A. I cannot recollect, but believe about the turn of the day.

Q. If the music of the rebel camp had been sent to meet the Ballymanus corps and play them in, must you not have heard it?

A. The music of the camp was so constantly employed that I cannot recollect whether they played or went to meet prisoner upon his coming in.

Q. About what hour did the rebel army march from Kilcavan to Carrigrua?

A. About nightfall.

Q. Do you not mean that when you saw prisoner with Major Fitzgerald at Blackwater, (listing) he was raising recruits for His Majesty's service?

A.   I did mean so.


John Carty sworn

He identified the prisoner.  He was called out of bed the night but one before the battle of Arklow and told that if he did not go to Gorey Hill and join the rebel army, he would be killed by the army. He accordingly got up and went to the rebel camp.

He was in a company called the Arklow Northshire, commanded by one Matthew Doyle as Captain, which company when the rebel army marched to attack Arklow was included in the corps called the Ballymanus corps, commanded by the prisoner William Byrne or by Perry.  He did not hear of any body or corps of county of Wicklow men, except those which were included in the Ballymanus corps.  He did suppose that the prisoner William Byrne or Perry commanded the Ballymanus corps, because they rode at the head on the march to Arklow.

Heard Perry called Captain and also heard the prisoner called Captain Byrne, but did not hear either of them give any orders as he was far in the rear.

Father Murphy, before the rebel army left Gorey, assured the people that they would not be hurt by the balls from the King's army, and when witness came to the battle of Arklow, he had a good opinion of what the priest said until he saw some men killed near him.

When the rebel army went to Limerick Hill after the battle of Arklow, between 30 and 50 horsemen were assembled in a kind of ring when one of them said with an oath that the prisoner William Byrne ought to be piked to death on the hill rather than any other man, for they had not luck or grace since he joined them; and then another replied, "what could be expected of him but treachery, as the rest of his family were guilty of".  Witness, in order to put prisoner upon his guard, informed one of Ballymanus's men of what he heard and desired him to tell prisoner.

Witness does not know what act of treachery the foregoing declaration alluded to.

*Cross-examined by the Prisoner*

Q.  At what time, to the best of your knowledge, did the Ballymanus corps march into the camp at Gorey Hill?

A.  I do not know.

Q.  Who carried the colours of the Ballymanus corps?

A.  I do not know.

Q.  Did you know or hear of Michael Reynolds of Naas in the rebel camp?

A.  Not to my knowledge.

Q.  Did you know or hear of young Byrne, son of Peter Byrne of Ballykaskan near Rathdrum, in the rebel camp?

A.  I do not recollect.

Q.  Were there not several horsemen riding with the rebel army on the march from Gorey to Arklow, and were there not many horsemen riding before the Ballymanus corps on that march?

A.  There were a great many horsemen with the army, and I believe several rode at the head of the Ballymanus corps.


# Patrick Harold,
## brought in by military force, sworn

Witness was out with the rebels in the Redcross company, commanded by Captain Charles Byrne of Ballyrogan. He was at Gorey Hill when prisoner marched in at the head of about 200 men, called the Ballymanus corps, of which prisoner was called Captain.

-      that the next day the rebel army marched to the attack of Arklow and the Ballymanus corps, in which Charles Byrne's company, which then consisted of 30 or 40 men, was included, was commanded by prisoner William Byrne, and believes all the county of Wicklow men were included in the name of the Ballymanus corps and commanded by the prisoner.

-      that he saw the prisoner at the battle of Arklow rally his men and bring them up to renew the atack.

-      that he saw Mr. Bayley's house near Arklow on fire that day, and understood that it was burned by order of Perry and prisoner.

-      did not see or hear any person having the command of the county of Wicklow men but the prisoner.

-   the rebel army returned through Gorey to Gorey Hill, and heard that Langrell and Wheatley were piked in the churchyard of Gorey, but was not present.
-   the rebel army marched to Limerick Hill and to Mount Pleasant where witness saw the prisoner and understood he still continued in the command of the county of Wicklow men. Two men were brought into the camp and shot at Mount Pleasant because they were two Orange-men; another man was taken afterwards and let go; he saw William Dowse, a prisoner, and some old men.
-   the rebel army marched to Kilcavan where prisoner kept the same command and afterwards marched to Vinegar Hill where all the county of Wicklow men were known and called by the appellation of the Ballymanus corps.
-   he did not see the prisoner at Vinegar Hill, but heard a dispute had arisen between Kyan and prisoner about an order for the march of the Ballymanus corps towards Enniscorthy.

*Cross-examined by Prisoner*
Q.   Were not the Captains of rebels appointed to their command some time before the rebellion, and were they not employed for a considerable time in disciplining their men?
A.   I do not know.
Q.   On what day and at what time of the day did you see the prisoner ride with the Ballymanus corps into the rebel camp?
A.   It was about the middle of the day he marched in and, as I think, about 4 or 5 days before the battle of Arklow.
Q.   Were you ever accused of robbing the widow Murray's house near Arklow?
A.   I was.


# Mathew Davis
## likewise brought in by military guard, sworn

Knows the prisoner. Witness was in a rebel company, in which James Doyle of Ballynecore was Captain, and went to join the rebel army at Mount Pleasant.

- the company then consisted of about 40 men, but was not complete. Patrick Grant, Dwyer, and one James Devitt were also Captains, and at Mount Pleasant also.
- all the county Wicklow men joined the Ballymanus corps and were commanded by the prisoner William Byrne
- that three men were brought into the camp at Mount Pleasant and these men were shot, as being Orange-men, by Captain Dwyer, but none of the head commanders were present. By head conmmanders I mean Perry, Kyan, the prisoner, and some others.
- that there was a piece of brass cannon, which was called Captain Byrne's cannon, it was short with wide bore. Saw the prisoner fire this cannon at the King's forces, which approached the rebels.
- that he afterwards saw the prisoner at Kilcavan, upon the appearance of the King's army draw out into ranks the Ballymanus corps in which Captain James Doyle's and Grant's companies, as he believes all the other county Wicklow companies, were included. Witness heard prisoner give them the word of command.
- that the rebel army went to Vinegar Hill, where the county of Wicklow men were under the command of the prisoner.
- that the county Wicklow men were ordered down into Enniscorthy, they marched part of the way, but finding their commander, William Byrne the prisoner, did not head them, they refused to proceed without him. The county Wicklowmen went to Enniscorthy with Kyan but soon after returned towards the hill and as they went there they met the prisoner who, as their commander, led them down again to Enniscorthy. The party were soon after ordered back up the hill, where they were dispersed by the King's army.

*Cross-examined by Prisoner*

Q. Who carried the colours of the Ballymanus corps?
A. I cannot tell.
Q. Did you know or see a man called Michael Reynolds in the rebel camp? Had he any command there, and what was his corps called?
A. I never did, but heard one Reynolds was at the battle of Hacketstown. I was not there myself.

Q. Did you know or see any person of the name of Kerevan in the rebel army? Had he any command, and of what corps?

A. I did not. There might have been private men of his name, but he (sic) never heard of a Captain of that name.

Q. Was Garret Byrne, prisoner's brother, at Kilcavan, Gorey or Vinegar Hill?

A. I was not at Gorey. I did not see Garret Byrne at Kilcavan or Vinegar Hill.

## Joseph Gordon sworn

Witness was a prisoner in the rebel camp on Gorey Hill. Saw the prisoner there commanding a great number of men, about three or 400 who were called the Ballymanus corps, and ordering to march and wheel and so on. Prisoner was called Captain Byrne and rode with a sword in his hand.

*Cross-examined by Prisoner*

Q. On what day and at about what time of day did you see the prisoner at Gorey Hill?

A. It was about 12 o'clock in the day, and thinks it was two days before the battle of Arklow.

Q. In what place were you confined, and were any persons, and what were their names, confined in the same place with you?

A. Sometimes on the hill and sometimes in Gorey. Arthur Spencer, Ed. Webster and others were prisoners also.

Q. Did you leave Gorey Hill on Friday before the battle of Arklow, when you got your protection from Perry?

A. I did.

Q. About what hour on Friday did you leave Gorey Hill, and did you see the prisoner commanding his men on any day before Friday?

A. I was not at Gorey Hill that day at the time of the parade and, as I said before, it was the day before I saw the prisoner exercise his men.

*By the Court*

Q. Are you now positive that you saw the prisoner at any time exercise his men on Gorey Hill?

A.  I am positive.

## Thomas Hugo, Esq
## again called by the prisoner

Q.  How many Roman Catholics were in your corps at the time the prisoner was expelled, and what is his religion as you have heard and believe?

A.  Prisoner is a Catholic, there were three including the prisoner as I believe.

Q.  Do you not believe that a man of the prisoner's rank and religion in the country, who was not at the commencement of the rebellion a member of any military body, would therefore be suspected of disloyalty?

A.  Yes I would.

*By the Court*

Q.  Did you hear the prisoner at any time before the prisoner was expelled from the Wicklow cavalry, say at your table that the King's forces consisted of no more than 75,000 men, regulars, militia, yeomen, and of them some of the militia would desert?

A.  I did, and prisoner further said, what signified that handful to the other force which consisted of 300,000 - at that time I had a good opinion of prisoner and therefore his assertion did not make much impression on me.

Q.  Had not the prisoner early information respecting any event, or pretended to have such information?

A.  I remember returning from Dublin home with Mr. Critchley, when I found prisoner at dinner at his house.  Prisoner asked Mr. Critchley what news? Critchley said none and asked Byrne had he any news. Prisoner said he had very bad, for the canal boat going to Athy had been plundered of a considerable number of arms belonging to his Majesty.  I was but a few hours returning from Dublin and I had not heard of the transaction there, and therefore believed prisoner received his information across the mountains.

Q.  Did you hear, or do you believe, the prisoner influenced any, and what number of persons, to join the rebel army?

A.  I did hear, and do believe he influenced many.

# PRISONER PUT ON HIS DEFENCE

*Prisoner to Captain Carroll, a Member of the Court*

Q. Did you give the prisoner leave to take a copy of the oath which the members of your corps proposed to take, with permission to consider it until the Sunday following?

A. I did give such permission, and some days to consider of the oath.

Q. Was the prisoner expelled on the Sunday following, and before he gave his answer?

A. I do not recollect that the prisoner was expelled on the Sunday following, but it was not before he gave his answer, which was that he would swear that he was not a United Irishman, but that he would not swear what he might thereafter be.

Q. Do you not think that if the prisoner had been a United Irishman, he would have the same objection to the former as to the latter part of the oath?

A. I should suppose so.

*By the Court*

Q. Do you think the prisoner's principles as to loyalty or sedition were changed by being expelled, and if he had any traitorous intentions whether he would not have wished to continue a yeoman, the better to conceal them?

A. I think the prisoner was a seditious man at the time he was expelled, and I think he would have wished to continue a yeoman to conceal his intentions.

Q. Whether if he had been a yeoman at the time of the battle of Clough, he would not in consequence of the success of the rebels, have deserted his corps to join?

A. I believe every disloyal man would take the first opportunity to join his party, and I believe the prisoner was a disloyal man.

## Captain King
### a member of the court, by prisoner sworn

Q. Are you a Captain of any, and what corps of yeomen? And did the prisoner at any time and after the rebellion commenced, in Mr.

Bates's parlour in Rathdrum, apply to you to bear arms, under your command? Did you give the prisoner any certificate and of what nature?

A. I am Captain of the Rathdrum cavalry. I recollect that after some days of the breaking out of the rebellion, the prisoner came to Rathdrum and met Captain Mills and me, who were both magistrates of this county, and prisoner having stated that several reports had been propogated to his prejudice, as a loyal man, requested to know if any charge had been made before us against him of a seditious nature, and he being answered that there had not, the prisoner said he hoped that we would have no objection to give him a certificate to that effect, which was complied with. I do not recollect the prisoner asking to be admitted into my corps, but if he did make such application I am confident he would not have been admitted.

## Mrs. Bridget Meagher sworn

Knows the prisoner. Saw him at the camp at Mount Pleasant, where she went in order to make interest to get off Mr. Thomas Dowse, Marks Redmond and one Myers, who were prisoners there.

- that she applied to the prisoner William Byrne for that purpose, supposing that from his rank and influence in the country, he could set them at liberty. Prisoner told witness that he had done his utmost but could not succeed, and then one Reynolds, who witness heard was a staff officer, and was then in the tent with Mr. Dowse, said that prisoner had no power there, and witness could not succeed in liberating Dowse. Witness believes that from the character of the prisoner, and from what she there observed, that he would have been more inclined to liberate the prisoners than detain them, and that his not releasing them proceeded not from want of willingness, but want of power.

- prisoner was more meanly dressed at Mount Pleasant than she had ever seen him. She did not see any badge or distinctive mark to induce her to believe he was a leader of the rebel army. She heard he had been sick the night before but appeared at that time well.

-   she went to Mount Pleasant about one o'clock and remained there until about five or six. She saw Captain Perry there, also Esmond Kyan and five or six other officers. Those officers were well dressed, and most of them wore scarlet and green; some had green sashes and cockades. She heard Perry called Captain, three or four more seemed to have equal power with him. She did not hear prisoner called by any other appellation on that place than that of Mr. Byrne.

-   she was at Mount Pleasant when the King's army attacked the rebels. She observed among the rebels a body of men called the Ballymanus corps, and did not see the prisoner take any command over that corps, or in the rebel army upon that occasion, and had an opportunity of seeing the prisoner if he had taken any command and saw him every quarter of an hour during the action. She heard a cannon fired from the rebel army against the King's troops. The prisoner was in her sight, either a little before or a little after the cannon was fired. He came to witness after the cannon was fired and advised witness to get home as fast as she could and he came part of the way with her. There was only one report but believes two cannon were fired. She heard prisoner was a relation of Esmond Kyan.

*Bridget Meagher cross-examined (by the Court)*

Q. You said you went to the rebel camp to get off Mr. Dowse and other loyal prisoners. Who acquainted you and how did you know there were any loyal prisoners in the rebel camp, did they or any of theirs apply to you to get them liberated?

A. The wife of Marks Redmond and the daughter of Myers applied to me for that purpose, but Mr. Dowse did not.

Q. You said the prisoner was the first you applied to on your arrival there and did he not go with you to Captain Perry and the other rebel leaders, and what conversation passed?

A. Prisoner did go with me to Captain Perry to whom I applied to release Mr. Dowse, who I represented as a very good man in the country. Captain Perry answered that he would speak for him and then rode up to the other rebel leaders, two of whom were called Fitzgerald and Redmond. Mr. Perry then rode off among the other rebel leaders and prisoner went with me to the marquee where Dowse was confined and where Reynolds was.

Q. If prisoner had not a mind to liberate prisoner Dowse and the other prisoners, would it not be more likely to throw the refusal upon Reynolds, or some of the other leaders than he himself under the disagreeable necessity of refusing an old friend.

A. I believe he would have refused to put the refusal off himself than have given me a denial, but I believe prisoner did endeavour to get off Dowse.

Q. Were you not on a friendly footing with Captain Perry, and when he said he would go to the other gentlemen to speak for Dowse, did you not think he wished to put the refusal off himself?

A. Captain Perry was on a friendly footing with me. He was a complaisant gentleman who did not chose to say "I won't", and I believe if Captain Perry had a mind he could have released Dowse.

Q. Had you any other inducement to visit the rebel camp, a place at the time you went there full of riot, confusion and danger?

A. I had no other motive.

Q. Had you or your husband any, and how many, relations at that time in the rebel camp, and who by name?

A. My son-in-law Daniel Kerevan was in the rebel army, but not in the camp that day, he was at my house at Coolelug, distant about two miles from the camp.

Q. How was the prisoner dressed?

A. He had a grey great coat and boots, but I did not see a sword.

Q. Who went with you to the camp?

A. Three children and a servant.

Q. How many of prisoner's men came to your house the night before you went to the camp?

A. One Neal from Ballymanus came in about break of day in the morning to enquire for prisoner, there were five or 6 others remained without. Neal was tenant to prisoner or his brother.

Q. Did you hear that your son-in-law Daniel Kerevan was killed in the rebel army at Vinegar Hill, and whether you did not hear something of the prisoner upon that occasion, and what was it?

A. I did hear from some of the poor people who returned from Vinegar Hill, and who called prisoner Captain, that Kerevan was killed there, and that the prisoner there left his men, and that Kerevan was thereupon appointed to the command in the place of the prisoner. I heard that the prisoner was charged with cowardice, and that he ran away.

*By the Prisoner*
Q.  How far from Ballymanus did Kerevan live?
A.  About five miles.


## Bridget Loftus sworn

Lives at Annacurragh and about two miles distant from and in the same parish with Ballymanus. Knows the prisoner, recollects seeing him the Thursday before the battle of Arklow at prayers in the chapel at Annacurragh. A man with green boughs in his hat came there, and afterwards heard some of the mass people tell the prisoner that said man came to warn them to join the rebel army at Kilcavan gap, and asked prisoner would he join them. He answered he would not.

Prisoner then went into her father's house. Some of the mass people again asked prisoner to go with them. He said they were very foolish people, they did not look to what they were going to do, it was not to an inn(?) or place of diversion. They turned out of the house and said he was a cowardly rascal, and if he would not join them they would make an example of him in the county of Wicklow. Witness went and told prisoner what she had heard. The evening following, which was that of Friday, witness saw prisoner at her father's near sunset. Witness asked him what news. He said he had made his escape from the cavalry. He had stopped at Mr. Coates's at Clone the night before. He, the prisoner, had sent a note by his servant to Clone, and said servant not having returned, prisoner said if he had any person to go with him he would go in search of his mare as he feared his servant had gone off with her. Prisoner and witness's father then rode away. Witness heard that prisoner spent Friday, until he came to her father's, in a gravel hole at Ballymanus.

It did not appear, from what she saw on Thursday at the chapel, that prisoner had command over them or had any authority, nor was he considered an officer, and never heard him called Captain. She has reason to know or believe that a corps called the Ballymanus corps left her neighbourhood. She saw some of Ballymanus corps march to the rebel camp. Never saw prisoner assume any command over that corps.

*Cross-examined*

Q. Are you related to the prisoner, and in what degree?

A. My father and prisoner's father were cousin germans.

Q. Did you know one William Michael Byrne, and was he a relation, and related to the prisoner?

A. He was our relation.

Q. Did you know Richard Reilly, and was he a relation and related to prisoner?

A. He was our relation.

Q. Did you know one William Young?

A. I did know him.

Q. Do you remember the last three persons meet at your father's house with some other persons?

A. I do. They met there before the rebellion.

Q. Did you hear for what purpose the meeting was held?

A. I heard, after they went away, that it was a meeting of United Irishmen, for the purpose of carrying on treasonable designs.

Q. Did you or your father give before a magistrate any information respecting that meeting?

A. I did not, nor did my father as I believe.

Q. Was there any meeting of the same kind at any time since held at your father's house?

A. One evening another party met, which I suspected was a meeting of the same kind; some of the persons who were at the first meeting were at the second.

Q. At what time did prisoner and your father leave your father's house and where did they go?

A. About sunset, but cannot tell where they went.

Q. How soon after did you see your father and prisoner?

A. My father returned home the day before the rebel army marched to Mount Pleasant, distant about five miles, and went back in about an hour. I did not see the prisoner since until I saw him in Wicklow. My father had a sword when he returned home. I heard prisoner was sick that day, but did not hear where he was.

Q. Did you hear the prisoner was at the battle of Arklow, and had a ball shot through his hat?

A. I did hear it.

Q. Did you hear that prisoner was at Vinegar Hill, and was your father reported to have been killed there?

A. I did hear so, and that my father was killed there.

Q. Did you hear that the prisoner was charged with cowardice at Vinegar Hill?

A. I did hear it.

Q. Did you ever see your father since the battle of Vinegar Hill?

A. I did not see him since.

## Michael Brennan sworn

Knows the prisoner from his infancy. Witness lives at Ballymanus. Saw the prisoner on the Friday next before the battle of Arklow on the lands of Ballymanus, both in the forenoon and in the afternoon. He was walking up the road from the big house, before the rebellion broke out. Prisoner desired witness to have a watchful look out about Ballymanus and that if he saw any people gathering to let the prisoner know, and that he, prisoner, would bring them before Captain King, a magistrate. This happened a few days before the battle of Arklow, particularly the day before prisoner desired witness to advise the tenants of Ballymanus to stay at home and behave themselves, and that would do best for them, and heard prisoner give same advice to some of the tenants. Witness never heard before the rebellion commenced that prisoner had any military command. Never at any time heard the prisoner called by the people of Ballymanus, or of the neighbourhood, Captain or any other military title.

*Cross-examined*

Q. Who are you tenant to?

A. Mr. Garret Byrne.

Q. Did the prisoner behave kindly to his brother's tenantry, and was he considered by them as their friend, and in consequence had he not a great influence over them?

A. Prisoner did behave kindly to his brother's tenantry, and was considered as their friend, and I think he had influence over them.

Q. How many tenants, old and young men, were there on Ballymanus?

A. About thirty-two.

Q. How many of those did not, as you heard and believe, join in the rebellion?

A. I believe about half the number of tenants went off as rebels.

Q. How many of the real inhabitants of Ballymanus did you hear were at the battle of Arklow?

A. About sixteen.

Q. Did you hear that at the battle of Arklow there was a numerous corps called the Ballymanus corps?

A. I did.

Q. Who commanded that corps at the battle of Arklow?

A. Daniel Kerevan.

Q. Were you ever sworn a United Irishman?

A. I was, but do not recollect what the oath was.

Q. Did you mean to keep that oath?

A. I did not mean to keep it.

Q. Did you inform any magistrates of your being forced to take that oath?

A. I did not.

Q. You have said that the prisoner had an influence over his brother's tenantry. Now, do you believe if prisoner had exerted that influence fully, he could not have prevented that tenantry from joining in the rebellion?

A. I do not believe he could have prevented those who went out.

*Question desired by Prisoner to be put to Witness*

Q. Do you believe that those of the tenantry of Ballymanus who were rebels were made such by the influence of the prisoner?

A. I believe they were not.

*July 1st:*          Martin Roche sworn

Knows the prisoner since he was a child. Witness lives in Ballymanus. He remembers that before the rebellion prisoner advised him and the other tenants to stay at home and mind their houses. Never heard prisoner advise the tenants to rise in rebellion. Nor ever saw or heard that the prisoner took any command among the tenants of Ballymanus as a rebel leader.

On the Friday before, which was the day next before the battle of Arklow, he saw the prisoner about two o'clock in the day, and saw him about seven o'clock that evening. Prisoner lay in a water cut on witness's land a good part of the forenoon on said day, where witness saw him and heard prisoner advise the people to stay at home, and that for his part he did not know where to go or what to do.

## Cross-examined

Witness admits he was a United Irishman. Never heard that more than six Ballymanus men went out at first and two afterwards, and that three or four went out occasionally. Eight are still absent from the town. Heard and believes that prisoner was at the battle of Arklow and shot through the hat.

Prisoner the night before the battle rode off towards Killiduff which was the road to Arklow about half after seven in the evening. He rode a bay mare which was the only one he had at that time.

While he remained at Ballymanus that day, his mare was at Neal's house, who was considered the greatest rebel in Ballymanus.

About two o'clock, prisoner told witness that he was hunted by the cavalry of Killacloran through Upper Aughrim, Craffield and to Ballymanus and thought it necessary to hide in the watercut. If the prisoner gave witness a true account of the time he took when he was hunted by the cavalry, prisoner must have left Annacurragh bridge behind him - Miss Loftus lives in Annacurragh. Witness understood that it was very early when prisoner was hunted by the cavalry; never heard who the cavalry were.

He cannot tell whether the prisoner exerted his influence over Ballymanus tenants, all of them that did go out would have gone or not. He heard that Daniel Kerevan commanded the Ballymanus corps at the battle of Arklow, that is, that he was Captain of a company of the Ballymanus district, but whether he commanded any other county Wicklow company he never heard. Never heard that the prisoner was called Captain and heard that Daniel Kerevan commanded the Ballymanus Company at Vinegar Hill. Heard that the prisoner had been charged with cowardice, but did not hear upon what occasion.

## Lieutenant Edward Hogg
## of the Antrim Militia, sworn

Witness was taken prisoner at Clogh on the 4th of June, was in Gorey on the 8th; saw prisoner on Gorey Hill on the 10th. Prisoner came forward and saved witness and others of the King's troops from being put to death. It did not appear to witness whether prisoner had or had not any command in the rebel army; if he had not a command he had considerable influence. Prisoner was not in coloured cloaths.

- never heard the prisoner in his, the prisoner's, presence called Captain, or by any other military appellation. Never heard any of the other rebel leaders call him Captain.

- witness was in Wexford gaol on the day of the battle of Vinegar Hill.

- saw Esmond Kyan about five o'clock in the morning of that day in the gaol of Wexford. He does not know whether Esmond Kyan could or could not have been at the battle of Vinegar Hill, which is about 11 miles from Wexford.

- witness, from what he observed of the prisoner while with the rebels and saving his, witness's, life rather thinks that he would save the life of a protestant prisoner than assist in his murder.

*Cross-examined*

Witness having been observed speaking to some of the Antrim soldiers, who were prisoners, some of the rebel guard who was placed over witness, said he ought to be piked and came forward, as he believes, for that purpose. Esmond Kyan was at a little distance but did not interfer. Did not see any other rebel officer there that he knew. Prisoner then interferred in behalf of witness and took him down to Gorey and after some time put him under a guard.

Believes that it was the custom of the rebel leaders to endeavour to prevail upon the militia officers and privates to join their party, rather than to put them to death; and that they hoped if they could get over an officer that privates would follow.

Witness himself was pressed to go over.

The vengence of the rebels was more directed against the yeomanry and loyal protestant inhabitants, particularly those called or suspected of being Orange-men, than the military.

Witness saw several of the rebel leaders in coloured cloaths and some of them without any badge of distinction. The rebel chiefs prevailed more upon the common men by persuasion than by peremptory orders.

Did never hear that the prisoner was at the battle of Arklow.

*Question by prisoner*

Q. Supposing prisoner did not have a command, do you not think his rank in life would have given him sufficient influence among the lower class of rebels to procure your liberation?

A. It appeared so that day.

*Question by the Court*

Q. Then why did not prisoner liberate you entirely?

A. I do not know, but suppose Esmond Kyan, who was called General, had a greater power than prisoner, and I believe that I was detained by his order and continued in custody until after the battle of Vinegar Hill.

Prisoner did not to my knowledge apply to Kyan to liberate me.

Two of the Antrim sergeants who were prisoners with the rebels, and were compelled to work the rebel guns, and who afterwards rejoined the regiment often told me that prisoner was a rebel leader, and I believe what they told me.

# Defence of William Byrne, Esq

Mr. President and Gentlemen of the Court,

Among the many embarrassments of my present situation, I lament as one of the greatest not merely the magnitude but the number of crimes of which I am accused.

It has been deemed proper to lay to my charge every offence to which the clemency of the Crown and the wisdom of Parliament have thought it expedient not to extend amnesty or pardon. The highest degrees of political as well as moral guilt are imputed to me, and I am now called on to defend myself against the complicated crime of disloyalty, aggravated by desertion, and blackened by murder. One great disadvantage attending a charge which contains such a variety of offences must occur to every mind.

It is obvious that the difficulty of defence is increased in proper proportion to the generality and indefiniteness of the accusation and that it might not be easy for even innocence to protect itself against the charge of a multitude of crimes, where it is impossible to foresee to which the evidence will be principally directed, or by what witness it is intended to be sustained.

Give me leave also to say that this observation is peculiarly applicable to the situation in which I stand since it is well known that a long time has been consumed, and much effort used, in the preparing of this prosecution, and that the day I was called to my trial was the first on which I had notice of the precise offence of which I was to be accused.

I may further observe that the enormity, added to the number of my imputed offences, must have a necessary tendency to excite prejudice and rouse indignation against one, whom the law of reason and the law of the land supposed before conviction to be innocent.

But it is only among those who are not my judges that I have any apprehension of unfounded prejudice and improper feeling; and I willing seek refuge and protection from the calumny of my enemies in the honour and integrity of this court.

In that candour and uprightness which has marked this trial through every step of its progress, and which (if I maybe permitted to particularize) has conspicuously appeared, Sir, in the patience, impartiality, and politeness of your conduct.

Before I proceed to my defence, it will, I hope, be permitted me to make another preliminary observation, which indeed arises out of the testimony of one of the last witnesses called in the prosecution. He said he lately saw me in the town of Blackwater, raising recruits for His Majesty's service. It is very true, for the crimes into which I was rather forced than betrayed, I have long felt the most sincere contrition. I have most faithfully returned to my allegiance, and so far from persevering in rebellion, my time has been actively employed in His Majesty's service. Surely I have some reason to say, that the zeal of my prosecutors, though honourable, was perhaps mistaken, because if they had permitted me to remain unmolested, it was my fixed determination that my life should be devoted to some useful occupation, and that my former errors should be amply atoned by the merits of my future conduct.

I lament that my criminality has been such as no repentance can wipe away, and that I am now brought to trial for offences which I fondly hoped were either overlooked or forgotten.

But it is in vain for me to deplore what I cannot prevent; and I have now no choice left, or duty to perform, but that of proceeding to defend myself against the heavy charge preferred against me. In doing so, I shall pursue the order observed in the charge. I begin with the imputed crime of desertion.

On this topic I might content myself with referring to the words of the amnesty act and the evidence of Mr. Hugo. Had there been any witness to prove the act of desertion, I should have appealed to the evidence of Mr. Hugo, and relied on it as decisive in my favour. The exception in the amnesty act, on which this charge is founded, is of such yeomen who have "deserted from their troops or companies and joined in the said horrid and unnatural rebellion". By the evidence it appears that, so far from deserting from my troop or company for the purpose of joining in rebellion in the month of February 1798, long before the rebellion broke out, I did not desert but was expelled from the corps of which I had been a member. The opinion of Mr. Hugo was, indeed, taken whether I did not desert from the cause of loyalty; but surely it will be obvious that the desertion meant by the Legislature as applied to a yeoman signified the wilful flying from the King's ranks to the standard of rebellion.

I cannot, however, close this part of my defence without adverting to that oath which was the cause of my expulsion.

I am convinced that oath was proposed in the zeal and ardour of loyalty, but I may be allowed to say, that there was some hardship in being branded as a traitor for not taking a voluntary oath, which should have been a matter of choice, and which never was prescribed by the Legislature. Besides, although it is a certain truth that no oath forcibly imposed has a binding obligation, yet there is a wide difference between the taking, without observing such oath, and the taking a voluntary oath which professes to bind against the future taking of any traitorous oath, whether freely or by force, or which is nearly the same, makes no distinction between them. This is promising more perhaps than a scrupulous man could promise. In these observations on that oath I may be mistaken, and it may, and (from the character of most of those who took it) most likely is unexceptional, yet it is enough for me to say that in refusing to take it a scrupulous man might be mistaken without being disloyal. This, indeed, I know in my own person.

When the oath was proposed, his Majesty had not a more faithful subject than I was, but in consequence of my declining to take it, I was abandoned by my friends and stigmatised as a traitor. From this period I date the origin of all my errors and misfortunes.

I proceed to the second charge, namely, that during the rebellion I was a Captain in the army of the rebels.

To this point the evidence has been chiefly directed and, in considering that evidence, I shall not take each witness in the order in which he was called, but I shall endeavour to class and arrange such as spoke to the same facts, and compare their testimony. There are some of those witnesses, however, who have sworn on facts in which they are not only not corroborated, but in almost every particular contradicted by the others. These cannot be classed, and the first of this kind whom I shall notice is Bridget Dolan.

The court will recollect not only the character which this witness gave of herself, but also her conduct on the table. A girl of 18, flying from her friends and family, and joining a rabble of men for no other purpose and with no other hope than that of plunder; on a sudden embarking in all their wickedness, and chosen as the most bold and forward to do every act of mischief; bearing their firebrands, and choosing to be present at a barbarous murder as at an amusing spectacle. This court saw that monster of immorality, whose heart is not only divested of all the softness of her sex but of every sentiment of humanity, bear testimony against my life, with as an indecent and idle a levity as when she confessed to have burned the King's baggage, or to have been at the murder of an Orange-man. The court saw the laugh with which her testimony was accompanied; that laugh which made one shudder to see human nature so depraved.

I pass to her evidence, which was consistent with her character, and inconsistent with everything else. She, and she alone, swears that when I came to the camp at Gorey Hill, all the music, drums, fifes, fidlers, and pipers went out to meet me, and this circumstance, which must have made an impression on every other person, was unobserved by the other witnesses who have sworn that they saw me ride into the camp at Gorey Hill; and it is also to be observed, that although this witness affects to be extremely minute in her evidence, yet she forgets what is now the principal subject of enquiry, and what must have made the greatest impression on the rebels in arms, namely, the time when succours which they deemed so important arrived in their camp. It is also to be observed that through the whole of this witness's testimony there was a manifest and eager desire to declare everything against me which betrayed her into many flagrant inconsistencies. Thus, she swore, that she never saw me exercise my men, but that I drew out my corps, that however she never saw me draw out my corps, but positively that I acted as Captain, although she was unable to mention any one fact from which this positive inference could be drawn.

The same anxiety to be minute, and the same manifest deviation from the truth, distinguishes her account of the battle of Arklow, in which (according to herself) she was not only an active warrior, but a calm and undisturbed observer. There she saw me as busy as possible, at the head of my own corps, which, if any conclusion can be formed from her evidence, continued a compact and unbroken body, where the commander had no occasion to give any other order than to march, and her positive evidence is, that although she had a full opportunity of seeing me during the whole battle, I did not rally any men, or act as Captain in any other manner than by ordering them to march. Thus the testimony of this woman differs most essentially from that of other witnesses who have been called on (by) the prosecution.

But the evidence of this witness does not end here. For some days she reposes after the fatigues of Arklow and she next meets with me at Kilcavan, where she sees what no other witness saw. It is her fortune to observe me riding about the ranks giving military orders; and on this point it is only necessary to say that Bridget Dolan is not only unconfirmed by the other witnesses, but so far as their having an equal opportunity of observing the same circumstance, and not having observed it, amounts to a contradiction (which it certainly does, their testimony directly militates against hers). But this witness accompanies the rebel army to Vinegar Hill and here also her mind continues undismayed by the horror of battle, and her attention remains fixed solely on my conduct. She sees me in the engagement, and she hears what no other person ever heard, a dispute whether the command of a body of men should be given to me or to Garret Byrne, who she swears was also there. Indeed, she has sworn as decidedly that Garret Byrne was not only at Vinegar Hill, but at Gorey, Kilcavan, and Mount Pleasant, as to any other circumstance of which she has given evidence. It is not necessary to say that this, as well as almost every other part of her evidence, is belied, not only by what has appeared on this trial, but by recent and notorious facts.

I will not follow any further the polluted stream of this woman's evidence. In every turn, through all its progress, I appeal to the good sense and honourable feelings of this court, if it has not been defiled by the basest malice, and blackened by the most apparent perjury.

I willingly dismiss the evidence of Bridget Dolan, and I proceed to make a very few remarks for the present on that of John Conyers, William Poole, and Joseph Gordon, whom I place in the same class, because they were, or declared themselves to have been, prisoners with the rebels on Gorey Hill before the battle of Arklow. I shall, however, first take the liberty of observing that where two or more witnesses on the same side dispose to transactions which have happened at the same time and their accounts are essentially different, the mind not knowing on which to rest must, to avoid being deceived, reject the evidence.

I apply this observation most particularly to the evidence of Joseph Gordon, who swears to facts to which no witness has sworn. Thus he says that he was a prisoner at large on Gorey Hill, and that he saw me ordering men to march, wheel and so on. I oppose this witness to all the others who have appeared in the prosecution, he swears positively, and the court repeatedly pressed him on the point, that he saw me act in the manner he described two days before the battle of Arklow, and that it could not have been on Friday, because on that morning early he left Gorey Hill, to which place he did not return until after the battle of Arklow. Thus the evidence of Gordon may be dismissed from the attention of the court, or that of those who swore that on Friday they saw me come to Gorey Hill must be discredited.

On the testimony of Poole, I shall make two observations for the present. The first is that Redmond, who was really a Captain in the rebel army, assumed upon himself that authority and as such wrote the protection which he handed to the witness, but when he says I signed my name he cannot say that I assumed any authority, or was called by any military title. On the contrary it was not my seeking, but that of some rebels who refused permission to the prisoners to pass without my leave. Suppose me to have no command and such an application made to me, it would be an act of inhumanity of which I am incapable to deny my signature on such an occasion. The next remark I shall make on the evidence of Poole is its strange and unaccountable inconsistency. He procures his pass on the evening, and this in consequence of the rebels who are near him, refusing to permit him to go without it; he makes no use of the pass that evening while those surround him, over whom my name was supposed to have an influence, but the witness waits until the next day, when another set of men over whom I might have no influence, surround him. He then leaves the rebel camp without showing his pass, and he is met by a pikeman who threatens his life, yet he never thinks of using his protection, which the day before was so important, but he falls on his knees and is saved, not by the authority by those whose names are signed on it, but by the clemency of the rebel. There is something so marvellous in this story, that the mind would deny its belief, even if a subsequent part of this witness's testimony did not entirely destroy his credit. I allude to his having sworn that this transaction happened on the 4th of

51

June, that is three days before the men whom I am supposed to have commanded came into the rebel camp, according to many of the witnesses for the prosecution, and four days before I joined the rebels, according to all the witnesses who have appeared on my behalf.

Thus of these three witnesses, two appear to be plainly unworthy of my belief, and the testimony of the third (whom I do not know) rests on his own credit entirely, as the protection of which he has spoken has not been produced in evidence, or my handwriting to it proved. However, supposing, but not admitting, the truth of what Conyers has said, I hope to show hereafter that it may admit of explanation, without attaching to me the guilt of being a Captain of the rebels.

The next class of witnesses on whom I shall observe are Benjamin Warren, James Patchell, and Farmer.

My reason for placing these together is that they have sworn to the same facts, and so far as their evidence has gone to criminate me, I have only to observe that what they have sworn is not directed to the subject of the charge, nor does it prove any offence from which I am now called to exculpate myself. If guided by rashness or resentment; if my feelings torn and distracted by the novelty and the horror of my situation; if the conflict of despair and remorse threw my mind off its centre and hurried me into acts which at any other time my conscience would disapprove; if at such a period of agitation I struck that blow of which these witnesses have spoken, I can now only express my sincere contrition for such an offence, and I solemnly declare it has escaped my recollection.

But I may also be permitted that as the assault on Benjamin Warren forms no part of the charge against me, evidence should not have been admitted, so peculiarly calculated to inflame against me those whose reason should remain cool. I am sorry that there should have been mixed with the immediate subject of investigation matters which can serve no other end than to rouse against me the indignation of my Judges. Let me not be understood to say that such an effect has been produced. No. I should do injustice to this court not to acknowledge that I sincerely believe that they will impartially discriminate the applicable from the irrelevant evidence, and that they will suffer no improper bias to turn their understandings from the real points of enquiry.

It will not, however, be imputed to me as presumptuous that I have ventured to mention what appears to me the natural and almost necessary tendency of this evidence, while, however, I deprecate the effects which this evidence might produce so far as it is irrelevant, I beg leave to resort to it when applying to the accusation as most strongly, I might indeed say, conclusively in my favour, it is unnecessary to repeat the evidence and it will be sufficient to remind the court of the conduct of Monks and of myself, when this is supposed to have happened; and what is the conversation which takes place between us? Does Monks, who was an acknowledged Captain, address me or treat me as an equal? Does he recognise me as a leader or call me by that title? He assumes a power and authority over me to which I am obliged to submit; he makes me suffer the most abject humiliation; he compels me to fall on my knees and beg pardon, he behaves to me in every respect not as if we were equal, but as if (what really was the case) I were his inferior and he a haughty and unbending superior, who had ample power which he had means of enforcing. Do I, to rescue myself from so degrading a condition, assert my authority or assume my rank? Is it not incredible that, if at that time I had authority or rank, I would not at that moment claim the one and assert the other? But I do neither. I do not say that you are but a Captain and I have an equal rank. No. He arrogantly demands of me who and what are you? My answer is such as it is impossible an equal could give: I tell him: "One Byrne of Ballymanus". Allow me to say that this fact speaks more emphatically, that I had not the rank of Captain in the Rebel Army, than the opinion of all those who were prisoners there. Opinion founded on facts which admit of explanation may be mistaken, but a fact such as this, to which these witnesses have sworn, cannot err. It is also very necessary to be observed here, that from all the evidence which has been given on this trial, the inference to be drawn concerning Monks is that he was considered in the Rebel Army as one of the common Captains (as distinguished from the principal leaders) and it cannot therefore be said that I might have been a Captain and Monks in a higher rank.

Let me also here make another use of the testimony of Benjamin Warren, who swore he heard Monks and Perry called

Captain, but heard the title applied to no other person. Is it to be believed that had I been a Captain the same title would not have been applied to me in the presence of those prisoners and of those who were rebel leaders? No. But if I were not a Captain it is certain that those who were such would not permit me to be called by that appellation in their presence. It has indeed been said by Benjamin Warren that Monks threatened to strip me of my commission. On this I shall only observe that if our rank were equal it is absurd to suppose he could have such a power, but that neither of the other witnesses (Patchel or Farmer) mentioned these words, although they both positively swore that they heard, and repeated on this trial, every word that Monks said, and it is more probable that they could directly hear and remember the conversation than one in Warren's then situation. Thus, I trust it will appear to the Court, that so far as the testimony of these witnesses apply to the charge before the Court, it goes a considerable way to removing from me the imputation of having being a Captain of the Rebels.

The next witnesses on whose testimony I shall observe are Maurice Dark, Joshua Chase, Thomas Paslow and William Grimes. These persons profess to swear to the same transaction, and to their testimony, the observation which I made before is particularly applicable. On examining what they have said, it is impossible to discover consistency on any one point; and not only are they inconsistent with each other, some of them are inconsistent with themselves. Two points to which these witnesses have sworn are, first, the liberation of the prisoners; secondly, the expression which I am supposed to have used. As to both of which, although each of these witnesses admits that the others had as good an opportunity of seeing and hearing what passed as he had himself, yet the account which each has given is as dissimilar from that given by the others as if the transaction were not the same.

Thus, Dark swears that, although he had an opportunity, he did not hear me give any direction what should be done with the old men and the children. Chase swears, that upon my being asked by Mergin, what should be done with the prisoners I answered if you do not put them to death put them in the guard-house. The affair is very differently represented by Paslow who swears, that without any application being made to me, I pre-emptorily say: "Why don't you despatch the prisoners?". Grimes hears what none of the others heard, but what he swears they could have heard. He says I confined my thirst of blood to the children and ordered them to be murdered, saying: "Damn them, kill them, or do what you like with them". And he positively swears that I used no other expressions respecting the prisoners. Dark swears that a mad fellow called Bergin or Mergin was going to kill Chase. Chase swears it was Mergin and neither Paslow nor Grimes mention anything of the transaction. Dark says I put a sentry in place of Mergin over the prisoners, and not a word of this is sworn to by the rest. When Mergin was removed, it was sworn to by Dark that Kavanagh was chosen by the rest as sergeant and this because he who was in that situation was disposed to treat the prisoners with cruelty. This is in some measure confirmed by Chase, who swears to the disappointment of Mergin at not being permitted to murder his prisoners, and all this happens by my interference after having used the sanguinary expressions imputed to me by some of these witnesses.

I rely, not so much on the various accounts which these witnesses have given of expressions shocking to humanity, as on their utter inconsistency with every other part of the transaction. According to Chase, the mob and particularly Mergin was eager for blood and as Chase has said they *waited* till I should come up, yet after having come up and excited them towards butchery, the prisoners are spared, Mergin is enraged, and declares that he will resign his command. According to Dark's story I save Lewis and reprove Mergin; according to Chase I make a bloody speech to sanguinary men, and they desert the project which they had formed. According to Paslow and Grimes, I give a cruel order to ruffians who were panting for innocent blood and I am disobeyed. These are a few of the inconsistencies which appear on the evidence of these men. Indeed, I may with some confidence affirm that this evidence is disproved by every act during the rebellion which has or can be proved against me. If I, at any time, assumed authority where none was ever conferred on me, it was to spare and not to shed the blood of captives.

There is, however, in the testimony of Paslow one circumstance most important, as it confirms this general observation, that I never was called Captain by any person who had reason to know whether

I was such or not, and that the title was never applied to me in my presence. The circumstance I allude to is, that so far was Mergin (who was but a sergeant) from acknowledging me as Captain, he told me in the presence of the prisoners and many rebels that I had no command. It is also to be observed, although (as Dark swears) I was extremely enraged against Mergin, I yet assumed no power to change him as a guard, but Kavanagh was chosen by the rest to be sergeant.

Thus, in examining the testimony of these witnesses the mind knows not where to rest, but involved in contradiction and inconsistency, it has no means of avoiding the perplexity than by entirely rejecting the evidence.

The next witnesses whom I shall class are John Hopkins and Patrick Harrold, and I class them for this obvious reason - they were both rebels, one in Wexford and the other in the Redcross corps, and the evidence of both is merely to circumstances which have been mentioned by other witnesses.

The evidence of Hopkins, who swears merely to having heard me called Captain by some of the rebels signifies little, when it is considered that he was a perfect stranger to me; swears to no act of command; and was unacquainted with that party of rebels among whom I remained.

The evidence of Harrold deserves further consideration, because he belonged to a corps of Wicklow rebels, but in order to entirely discredit him, who admitted that he had been accused of robbery (you know, Sir, that I could not have asked him was he guilty), I need only observe that he positively swore it was a week, or at least five days, before the battle of Arklow when the Ballymanus corps, led by me, came into the camp at Gorey Hill. Is it necessary to observe on this flagrant falsehood?

The next witnesses I shall observe are John Carty and Mathew Davis, who swore that they were rebels in the Ballymanus corps, and in these men there is to be observed the same inconsistency with the other witnesses, and with each other, which has been noticed in the former classes of witnesses who have been called to the same facts.

Carty professes to have belonged to the Ballymanus corps, which he says was composed of many inferior corps, and if I had any command, it must follow from this man's evidence, that it was not over an inferior corps, but of a body composed of many others. Yet he sees me to do no one act of military authority, he sees me issue no orders, assume no command; but he concludes that I must have been a Captain, because I was riding and looked more a gentleman than the rest. Allow me to say, that this is the way in which any title applied to me by the rebels came to be conferred. They imagined that one in my rank and of my appearance could have been nothing less than Captain, but they knew little that my connection with them had been but recent and was compelled.

To the evidence of John Carty, I oppose that of Mathew Doyle, who had no better opportunity of knowing my rank or the circumstances to which he has sworn than John Carty had, yet he swears to my having fired at Mount Pleasant a cannon which was called mine. In this particular Davis is uncorroborated by any one of the many witnesses who have been called and who had an equal opportunity of knowing whether such a thing were there. Let me also observe, that not one of those who say they saw the Ballymanus corps have mentioned one syllable of cannon, many of the witnesses have claimed they never heard of any such thing as cannon called Captain Byrne's cannon. Besides this, witness is for another reason not to be believed. He has sworn that Kyan was active at Vinegar Hill at a time when a much more respectable witness has proved him to be in Wexford. I may venture to say that this witness, whose testimony is not only uncorroborated by others, but who has sworn what is not true, will receive but little credit from this court; and had not those witnesses whom I summoned been prevented by their false fears from attending, I would have had abundant proof of every part of his perjury. I shall, however, make this one observation. It seems to have been admitted by all the witnesses for the prosecution that Perry had a command in the rebel army composed of many subordinate corps. It has not been in proof who was the leader of that aggregate body which was composed of the different corps from Wicklow, but from the evidence of Carty, it may be fairly inferred that Perry had that command. The reason for drawing this inference is that it has not appeared what other principal command Perry could have had, and Carty has said that he could not be positive that Perry had the sole command of this body; and although the names of the inferior Captains are mentioned by these witnesses, yet mine has not been attached by them to any subordinate body in that great division of the rebel army.

On the evidence of John Walker, who swears that at Arklow he saw me rally my men, I shall beg leave to call the attention of the Court, not merely to his inconsistency, which discredits what he said on his direct examination, but on the important fact which he disclosed on his cross-examination. He saw me rally my men, yet in that immense multitude which his ignorance multiples to three or four hundred thousand, the fact is, and he admits it, the rabble scattered and each man fought for himself. There was no regularity, no discipline, and no man thought of remaining with the corps to which he belonged; yet, according to this witness, when 200 of this body, who were mixed and confounded in the mass, were flying with the multitude, I rally my men. In this story there is a wild and extravagant improbability, but is it not improbable that a man on horseback, without a command, should at such a time and in such a situation, endeavour to turn the flight of those with whom he was acting? And thus, even by giving credit to this incredible witness, the fact that he has sworn by no means amounts to any proof of the charge.

It remains for me only to notice the evidence of Mr. Dowse, and I cannot here avoid remarking the prejudice against me, amounting almost to a vindictive and resentful feeling, which has appeared in the evidence of several of these witnesses, who certainly were rather under some obligations of gratitude to me. Mr. Dowse saw in my conduct, while he was with the rebels, nothing but kindness to him and humanity to others; and yet he would not admit that his belief was I would rather assist a protestant prisoner in his escape than join in his murder. I, who in vain solicited his liberation; I, who at that very time was employed in his service with the benefactress of Dowse, who hazarded her own life to save his. I, who to vindicate my own character need scarcely do more than point to it, living in the person of this witness as the example of my humanity. As to the evidence of this man concerning my being Captain, I rely on it as infinitely more strong in my favour than against me. He thought I had more command than a common man, but he saw me do no act of military authority, and the two facts on which his belief rests, are his having (the evening before Mrs. Mahar came to Mount Pleasant) seen me in the carriage with Esmond Kyan, and his having observed me in a consultation.

As to the former of these facts, it is fully explained by the admission of this witness and the circumstances proved by Mrs. Mahar. Dowse believes if I were a relation of Mr. Kyan, and were in ill-health, he would permit me to travel in his carriage, and Mrs. Mahar proves that I was a relation, and in truth a near relation of Kyan, and on that evening I was so sick that some of my friends were afraid my life was in danger.

As to the consultation, from what Mr Dowse has said it is plain that this fact is too slight to furnish a ground of inference. He saw many persons there who, he said, perhaps might not be Captains. He mentions the names of very few of them, and among these few is one (Barny Murray) who was no Captain.

On such flimsy and inconclusive circumstances, it is sought to convict me of a capital offence, but let me appeal to Mr. Dowse in my favour. He verily believes I wished to serve, and that my not having done so proceeded from want of power, not from want of willingness; and in this he is confirmed by Mrs. Mahar, who says that my whole heart and soul were bent on serving him, yet I do not serve him by restoring his goods. And why? Because if I had ventured to do so, I would myself have been punished, but he believes if I were a Captain I would not be punished and instead of giving him a refusal, I tell him to apply to some man having command. How is it possible to reconcile this with the idea of my having at that time any thing like power or command in the rebel army?

Man is equally ostentatious of his power, and never such a hypocrite or so humble as entirely to hide it. But Mrs. Mahar confirms Dowse. She thought I might have had some authority, but Reynolds, who well knew, undeceived her and said I had none. I beg to observe further on Dowse, that he had a full opportunity, as also had Mrs. Mahar, of seeing all I did at Mount Pleasant while they were there, yet neither of them saw me assume any command, but Dowse saw me riding, as other horsemen did, irregularly along the ranks, and of these horsemen there were, as he says, twenty privates to one officer.

I have thus finished what I am afraid may be a tedious examination of the evidence that has been given; and I believe it will not be saying too much to observe that the testimony of many of those witnesses is inconsistent with probability and with what some of the others have sworn. I may also be allowed to say that what is least improbable may admit of explanation.

There are two methods in which it occurs to me this may be done. One, on the supposition of my *not* having been a rebel leader, the other supposing I was one. Reasoning in this matter you will see which supposition is attended with the greater difficulty. If a young and active man of a rank much superior to the peasantry and of a family whose influence was very great among the lower class, had for the first time, just on the eve of a battle, joined such a rabble as the rebel army was, it is natural to imagine: -

- that his influence would be increased by such conduct.
- that the mob, who were forever fond of conferring titles, would speak of him (as Mrs. Mahar has said) as Captain, or Honor, or by that title which was at that time most in favour with them.
- that this title would be more frequently applied to him by strangers and never in his presence.

It is also reasonable to suppose that he would be looked up to by the lower class and that they would willingly comply with any request he might make; and if he were a man of humanity, he would certainly use his influence to rescue prisoners from danger and confinement. For this purpose, he would not only make personal applications to the mob, but if his name bore any weight among them, he would not refuse a signature which might protect an innocent man's person. He would be treated with more respect than others by those officers who had principal command, and in a place where there was no order, discipline or regularity, it is most likely his advice would be asked, or his assistance taken in either making musters or in advising about a march, particularly if he were well acquainted with the country. In all this, there is no inconsistency or improbability.

But reverse the picture. Is it within the bounds of human probability: -

- that such a man should be a Captain in the rebel army, and no credible witness see him assume any military command?

-       that no title should be applied to him in his presence or by any person having a command?

-       that he should have the will without the power to oblige a friend, and refer that friend to someone having authority?

-       that before the rebellion and, indeed, after it commenced, he should remain at home persuading the people, at the hazard of his own life, not to rise in rebellion?

-       that he should fly to the rebels attended by only one man?

-       that in the only instance where he seemed to assume power, a man in the rank of sergeant (I allude to Mergin) should in direct terms say "You have no command"?

-       that one, who had no higher rank than Captain, should treat him with the most insulting indignity, and that he should not assert his title?

-       and that those in his neighbourhood should not have heard of his having command of the people of the neighbourhood?

All these are absurd inconsistencies which attend the supposition my having been a Captain of the rebels. While every act of mine that has been proved by any credible witness can easily and probably be reconciled with the supposition of my having had no command.

I pass to the last charge. I am accused of having murdered Langrell and three men on Mount Pleasant. This, certainly, as it is the crime most repugnant to my nature, I did think would never have been laid at my charge. I feel that the court do not consider me guilty of it, and I shall therefore be very short in my observations.

As to the murder of Langrell is it not enough to say the only witness who has spoken one syllable on the subject is that same Bridget Dolan, whose barefaced and disgusting perjury shocked every man who heard her evidence; give me leave to say also that her evidence is belied by every other part of my conduct. I must also most solemnly assure the Court, that until the charge was read in this Court, I had no idea of any such crime being imputed to me, that being perfectly innocent of this offence, it is impossible for me to know what persons were present at it, that even if I did know them they would be incompetent witnesses, and therefore I have no other way of disproving this evidence than by relying on the infamous character of the witness.

As to the murder of the three men, this is not only not proved to have been done by me, but it is proved even in the prosecution that it was committed by a man called Captain Dwyer, over whom I could have no influence or control. And that I may be allowed to lament that a charge so entirely unfounded and unsupported was preferred against me.

I have now noticed the greatest part of the evidence, and on the part of the prosecution with a few observations on that which has been given on my behalf I shall conclude. Allow me, however, to premise that the characters of both Mrs. Mahar and of Miss Loftus have remained, after the most minute scrutiny, unimpeached and above blame. In Mrs. Mahar you see a woman of wealth and respectability, exposing herself to danger for the safety of her friends.

Although it may have been true that two meetings of persons, whom Miss Loftus afterwards heard were delegates, took place at her father's house, yet surely this was no offence that could destroy her credit.

Allow me also to say that Brennan and Roach are as worthy of credit as those witnesses in the same rank of life who were called in the prosecution, and that none of the witnesses in the defence told either an inconsistent or improbable story. I beg leave in the first place to advert to the evidence which was given by Captain Carroll. He has given his belief, founded on a very sufficient reason, that in the month of February 1798, when the conspiracy of the United Irishmen was completely organized, I was not one. It is very true. And if such a negative were capable of proof, I would be able to prove that I never was a United Irishman. But after my expulsion from the Wicklow corps, my place of residence was in a part of the country which was peculiarly disturbed. So far, however, from my countenancing those who were inflaming the minds of the lower orders, my most sincere exertions were used in dissuading the people from engaging in the conspiracy. Even after the rebellion broke out my endeavours to keep the people at home and in peace were unceasing.

But I was myself suspected of disloyalty, and to remove that imputation from my character and to ensure safety of my own person, I offered myself to a magistrate to answer any charges that might be made against me and he gave me a certificate of innocence. This happened long after the rebellion commenced, but at that time and in that place to be suspected was to be guilty, and without ever having done one disloyal act, the king's troops pursued me for my life.

Even at this time, when I was forced to seek shelter in the ditches and gravel pits, the influence which I had among the people in my neighbourhood was exerted in advising them against rebellion, and only two days before the battle of Arklow, after having escaped from a party of cavalry, I raised against myself the resentment of those very persons whom I might have easily engaged in rebellion, by advising them not to join the rebels. On the night before the battle of Arklow, I fled from the pursuit of the king's troops to the rebels at Gorey. Among them I had no command. I never acted with them as a military leader, but I felt I had influence among them, which I never exerted but for the purpose of doing acts of kindness and humanity. If my being instrumental in saving the lives of seventeen of his majesty's army, and many private individuals, be considered as a conclusive proof of my being a Captain of rebels, I can only say that it is not, and that whatever my fate may be, I can never regret the having had it in my power to serve so many fellow-creatures.

This is the short and faithful history of my life during the rebellion, and it is confirmed by the testimony of the witnesses who have appeared on my behalf. Had those whom I summoned appeared also, they not only would have given what I have said full confirmation, but they would disproved many of the particulars which have been sworn against me.

I have now done. And with perfect reliance on this honourable Court, I commit my case to their justice, candour, and impartiality, confident that if they see even room for doubt, their judgement will be an acquittal.

*By the Lord Lieutenant General and General Governor of Ireland*
*CORNWALLIS*

Whereas, at a General Court Martial held at Wicklow, the 28th day of March [1], and continued by adjournment to the 2nd day of July, 1799, whereof Major John King, of the Fermanagh Regiment of Militia, is President. The Court being met and duly sworn, proceeded to the trial of William Byrne, charged: -

- that he, by his being a Yeoman in the Wicklow Yeoman Cavalry, and as such having taken the oath of allegiance prescribed for Yeomen, afterwards became a rebel, and joined the rebel army then in arms against the King and Government of Ireland
- that he was instrumental in calling and influencing into rebellion divers of His Majesty's subjects
- that he was a Captain or principal leader in the said rebel army
- the said William Bryne is also charged with being concerned, and an accessory, in the murder of Isaac Langrell, in Gorey in the month of June 1798, and also being concerned in the murder of three other persons at the rebel camp at Mount Pleasant, whose names are unknown

The Court having taken into consideration the whole of the evidence in support of the several charges preferred against the prisoner, William Byrne, and also the prisoner's defence, are of opinion as follows, viz.

- that the prisoner William Byrne, having been a member of the Yeoman Corps of Wicklow Cavalry, from which, as it appears to the Court, he was expelled before he was guilty of any overt act of rebellion, is not therefore precluded from the benefit of the general amnesty, and he is therefore acquitted as a Yeoman deserting to the rebels; yet his entering into a Yeomanry Corps, taking the oath of Allegiance, and receiving the King's pay for upwards of six months, is a great aggravation of his subsequent rebellious conduct
- the Court are of opinion that the Prisoner was present, and commanded the rebels who murdered Isaac Langrell; yet as it appeared in evidence that party was sent from Gorey Hill, by order of some chief rebel commander, it might possibly have happened that the prisoner acted under such order. He is therefore acquitted

of the murder, although the prisoner's conduct on the occasion is deemed highly blameable

-      with respect to the three murders at Mount Pleasant, the prisoner is acquitted, in as much as it does not appear that the prisoner had the chief command in that place.

-      upon the whole, the prisoner by his conduct at the murder of Langrell, in the guard-house at Gorey, and at Mount Pleasant, exhibited a vengeful and malignant mind, and the Court being decidedly of opinion that he acted as a Captain or principal rebel leader at the battles of Arklow and Vinegar Hill, and other places, the Court do adjudge that the said William Byrne shall suffer DEATH

The Court think it necessary to observe that the prisoner William Byrne had all the time allowed to call in his witnesses which he desired, and that he was offered warrants to bring in those who being summoned did not appear.

We, having taken the proceedings and sentence of the said General Court Martial into consideration, are pleased hereby to approve of and confirm the same, and do direct and require that you will cause the sentence of DEATH, pronounced by the Court against the prisoner, William Byrne, to be carried into due execution.
For doing whereof this shall be your warrant.

Given at His Majesty's Castle of Dublin, this 21st day of September 1799, by His Excellency's command,

GASPER ERCK

Lieut. Gen. Charles Eustace
etc, etc, etc,

Note:
1.   The trial commenced on June 24th.   Byrne was not even arrested until May 14th.

*COPY OF A MEMORIAL presented to his Excellency the Lord Lieutenant, by Eleanor Byrne and Frances Byrne, on behalf of their brother, William Byrne, of Ballymanus, Esq*

May it please your Excellency

We throw ourselves at your Excellency's feet in favour of an ill-fated brother, William Byrne, now, we hear, a convict in your gaol of Wicklow, whom the general prejudice of the times (but particularly of that quarter) we fear will overwhelm, if not prevented by the interposition of your Excellency's wonted clemency. We entertain *little doubt* but your humanity will induce you to spare a life on which depends, we may say, the existence, assuredly the protection, of two solitary females.

Should your Excellency be moved to our tears and prayers to treat him with mercy, we implore you not to liberate him in Wicklow or its vicinity, *as the inveteracy of a party there* is such as must be fatal to him. Your Excellency *will not* deem our apprehensions ill-founded, when we are informed and believe with truth, that an attempt, accompanied with much unseasonable insult (his circumstances considered) was made on his life in the gaol during the Assizes *by two Yeomen*. We, with the utmost regret, deplore our distance from the Marchioness of Buckingham, our only relative of consequence sufficient to give any weight to our application, independent of your Excellency's well-known clemency. We, with most fervent prayers for your Excellency's happiness, wait with anxious hearts for your Excellency's commands at the Petition-office.


ELEANOR BYRNE
FRANCES BYRNE

*Wicklow, August 21st, 1799*

Sir,

Agreeable to the orders I received, I herewith have the honour to enclose an investigation and a report on the petition of Eleanor and Frances Byrne, and stated such *facts*, and submitted such observations, as came within my knowledge, and which, I hope, will meet his Excellency's approbation.  I also trust and hope that the Fermanagh Regiment is honoured with such a share of his Excellency's confidence, as he supposes we will on every occasion implicity obey his orders, and that either here or wherever quartered, they would not suffer his Excellency's commands or determination, be what it would, in Byrne's case or any other, to be insulted or opposed by either party or prejudice.

I have the honour to be,
Sir,
Your Most obedient humble servant
JOHN CALDWELL
Lieut. Col. F.M.

*To Lieut. Col. Littlehales. etc, etc*

*Investigation and report on the petition on Eleanor and Frances Byrne, presented to His Excellency, the Lord Lieutenant.*

1st.  The complaint made in said petition, of an attempt made on the life of William Byrne, is false and groundless.  Byrne gratefully acknowledges to have received, since his confinement, every indulgence and kindness his situation would admit, and never the smallest insult excepting some abusive language from a yeoman, who, during the Assizes was permitted to see an acquaintance in the gaol, and who Byrne perceiving to be in liquor, retired to his room.  He informed his sisters by letter of this circumstance, and contradicted a report they had heard in Dublin of an attempt said to have been made on his life.

2nd. The inveterate private or public prejudice complained of, I have not observed, save *that* universal odium and indignation naturally arising in the public mind, and in the breasts of the loyal inhabitants of this district, who have to weep over the rapine, murder and bloodshed with which this country was overwhelmed and desolated by the exertions of this rebel chief. And this hostile opinion against him has certainly not been diminished by the result of his trial, which clearly and incontrovertibly confirmed his guilt, and proved in the strongest manner that William Byrne, at the head of the County Wicklow Rebels committed enormities, compared to which the crimes of those who have already suffered are trifling.

3rd. With respect to the claims of relationship made by Eleanor and Frances Byrne to the Marchioness of Buckingham, none can exist, they being no kindred whatever to the Byrnes of Cabinteely, and even *their* connection arose only from the late Mr. Byrne's father being married to the Marchioness's aunt. But even admitting the relationship to *exist*, and that however grateful to the excellent and humane heart of Lady Buckingham to relieve the distresses of others, I will take the liberty to say, that her Ladyship upon being informed of the *true* state of the case, would not be induced to intercede with so black and criminal a character as Byrne, who being not only covered himself, and convicted of rebellion and murder, has, by his example and influence, seduced a multitude of ignorant wretches into the same crimes, many of whom have in consequence suffered.

4th. Whatever protection or support these young women might have received from their brother some years since, I know not. It must, from his situation, have always been very slender at that period, and long prior to it. William Byrne lived with his brother Garret, who, about four years ago, turned him out of his house, and threatened to prosecute him. The said William took refuge at the house of Thomas Hugo, Esq, who received and entertained him, his horses and servant, in the most kind and hospitable manner, and where he resided until the outbreak of the rebellion; at which period he left Mr. Hugo's and became *all at once* very intimate with his brother Garret. In return for Mr. Hugo's most kind, friendly, and generous treatment, he seduced his servants, labourers and tenants, who made an attempt to murder their kind master and landlord, and family, and who after burning and destroying his house and property, joined the Ballymanus corps of rebels, where many of them were killed fighting against the king's troops.

I am also informed, from undoubted authority, that William Byrne gave particular orders to *his party* to burn the house of the Rev. Edward Bayley, the day of the battle of Arklow, The probable cause was that Mr Bayley had some years ago purchased part of the estate of Byrne's father, under a Decree of the Court of Chancery, and because of the zeal and activity of Mr. Bayley, as a magistrate, to suppress the rebellion, although his exertions were tempered with the greatest humanity and benevolence.


JOHN CALDWELL
Lieut. Col. Fermanagh Militia
Wicklow
August 21st, 1799

EPILOGUE

The execution of Billy Byrne was duly carried out on September 26th, 1799. He was taken from the prison and led to the place of execution at the other end of the town, presumably the Abbey grounds. In 1935 the following story was recorded by Padraig O Tuathail and published in *Bealoideas*.

"His brother Garret went to the king to seek his reprieve and got it, and when he landed back in Dublin, he got on his horse and he rode him in such a state to Wicklow town that when he lit off the horse the horse fell dead, and Billy was hanged one hour. They hung him one hour too soon, to get shut of him, and he was lying on the ground when Garret arrived with his reprieve. Garret looked at him, and he had to turn away, and he asked the Ballymanus neighbours did Billy die a man. They was all in tears, the whole county round, and they went to bring him home, and they told him he died a man, and they buried him in the Wicklow Protestant graveyard, but the Ballymanus neighbours stole him out of it by night a while after and brought him home and buried him at Rosahane along with the family where there is fourteen skulls in the Byrne vault in Rosahane graveyard."

This account, along with the ballad, made the tragedy of Byrne's death even more melodramatic. Of course, it's all nonsense. There was no reprieve and even if there had been Garret would not have been in a position to secure it. He was already in exile for his involvement in the rising. What is important is that in the popular imagination Billy's execution should not have taken place. The authorities just wanted *'to get shut of him'*. Most important of all, *'he died a man'*.

There is mystery surrounding the ultimate fate of his body. One story says it was tossed into the sea. The above recounts another supposition. In 1898, however, as part of the centenary commemorations, Miss C. M. Doyle, a distant relative of Bridget Loftus, told *The Wicklow Star* that she believed that the body was buried in the Abbey grounds and there it remains.

# INDEX

Hopkins, John: iii, 28-29, 56
Hugo, Thomas: 2-5, 34, 47, 68-69
Hume, W.H.: 5

JHS: 15

Kavanagh, ...: 22, 25, 55, 56
Kerevan, Daniel: 33, 38, 39, 42, 43
Kilcavan: passim
Killacloran: 43
Killiduff: 43
Kinch, ...: 25
King, Capt.: 2, 11, 35, 41
King, Major John: 2, 64
Kyan, Esmond: 14, 15, 16, 17, 23, 28, 31, 32, 37, 44, 45, 57, 59.

Langrell, Isaac: 2, 6, 11, 20, 31, 61, 64, 65
Leslie, Capt.: 2
Lewis, William: 22, 23, 55
Limerick Hill: 6, 13, 14, 16, 23, 29, 31
Loftus, Bridget: 39-41, 43, 62, 70

Mahar, see Meagher, Bridget
Manning, William: 8
M'Cormack, ...: 7
Meagher, Bridget: iii, 36-39, 59, 60, 62
Mergan/Mergen/Mergin:iii, 22, 23, 24, 25, 26, 27, 54-56, 61
Mernagh, ...: 12, 14, 23
Mills, Capt.: 36
Monaseed: 21
Moncks, Capt: 18, 19, 20, 53-54.
Monks see Moncks
Mount Pleasant: passim
Murphy, Capt.: 21
Murphy, Fr.: 20, 29
Murray, Barny: 16, 59
Murray, 'Widow': 31
Mt. Nebo: 20
Myers, William: 25, 36, 37

Neal, ...: 38, 43

Paslow, Thomas: 25, 26, 27, 54-56
Patchel, James: 19, 52-54
Perry, Anthony: passim
Philips, ...: 8
Pierce, Roger: 14, 17
Poole, William: 18, 50-52

Rathdrum: 7, 8, 10, 11, 30, 36
Redcross: 30, 56
Redmond, Marks: 22, 25, 36, 37
Redmond, P.: 12, 14, 18, 38, 51
Reilly, Richard: 40
Reynolds, Michael: 30, 32, 36, 37, 38, 59
Roach see Roche
Roche, Martin: 42-44, 62
Rockingham: 17

Spencer, Arthur: 33

Tinahealy, see Tinnehaly
Tinnehaly: 14, 17, 24, 25, 26
Toole, Johnny: 9
Toole, Fr.: 14
Tombreen: 9

Verdict: 64-65
Vinegar Hill: passim

Wainwright, ...: 8
Walker, John: 20-21, 58
Walpole, Col.: 7
Warren, Benjamin: 18-19, 52-54
Webster, Ed.: 33
Wexford : iv, 19, 44, 56, 57
Wheatley, ...: 20, 31
White, Dr.: 19
Whyte, ...: 17, 18
Williams, Richard: 25
Winslow, Lt.: 2

Young, William: 40

72